# THE WAY
# OF THE
# FATHER

# THE WAY
# OF THE
# FATHER

## LESSONS FROM MY DAD,
## TRUTHS ABOUT GOD

# MICHAEL W. SMITH

#### with ROBERT NOLAND

BOOKS

FRANKLIN, TENNESEE

# K-LOVE BOOKS

An imprint of EMF Publishing, LLC
5700 West Oaks Blvd
Rocklin, CA 95765

Unless otherwise indicated, all Scripture quotations are taken from the Holy
Bible, New Living Translation, copyright ©1996, 2004, 2015 by Tyndale House
Foundation. Used by permission of Tyndale House Publishers, Carol Stream,
Illinois 60188. All rights reserved.

Scripture quotations marked MSG are taken from THE MESSAGE, copyright
© 1993, 2002, 2018 by Eugene H. Peterson. Used by permission of NavPress,
represented by Tyndale House Publishers. All right reserved.

Scripture quotations marked NIV are taken from the Holy Bible, New
International Version®, NIV®. Copyright ©1973, 1978, 1984, 2011 by Biblica,
Inc.™ Used by permission of Zondervan. All rights reserved worldwide. www
.zondervan.com The "NIV" and "New International Version" are trademarks
registered in the United States Patent and Trademark Office by Biblica, Inc.™

Printed in the United States of America.

First edition: 2021
10 9 8 7 6 5 4 3 2 1

ISBN: 978-1-954201-02-6 (hardcover)
ISBN: 978-1-954201-04-0 (trade paper)
ISBN: 978-1-954201-03-3 (eBook)
ISBN: 978-1-954201-05-7 (audiobook)

Publisher's Cataloging-in-Publication data

Names: Smith, Michael W. (Michael Whitaker), 1957-, author. | Noland, Robert,
author.
Title: The way of the father : lessons from my dad , truths about God / Michael
W. Smith with Robert Noland.
Description: Nashville, TN: K-LOVE Books, 2021.
Identifiers: ISBN: 978-1-954201-02-6 (hardcover) | 978-1-954201-04-0 (paperback)
| 978-1-954201-03-3 (ebook) | 978-1-954201-05-7 (audio)
Subjects: LCSH Smith, Michael W. (Michael Whitaker), 1957- .| Contemporary
Christian musicians—United States—Biography. | Contemporary Christian
musicians—Religious life. | Christian life. | BISAC RELIGION / Christian
Living / Personal Memoirs | BIOGRAPHY & AUTOBIOGRAPHY / Religious
| BIOGRAPHY & AUTOBIOGRAPHY / Music
Classification: LCC ML420.S67195 2021 | DDC 277.3/0825/092–dc23

This book was developed, designed, and produced in partnership with Dexterity.
Book design by PerfecType, Nashville, TN
Cover design by Bruce Gore | Gore Studio, Inc.
Jacket front photo courtesy of WanderCreative. All other photos courtesy of the author.

To my father, Paul Smith
These pages are to honor the son, father, grandfather,
great-grandfather,
child of God, and Jesus-follower you were,
and how you always
led by example as a servant-leader
in everything you did.


To my Abba Father:
God is my strength, God is my song, and, yes!
God is my salvation.
*This* is the kind of God I have
and I'm telling the world!
*This* is the God of my father!
Exodus 15:2 MSG

*See how very much*
*our Father loves us,*
*for he calls us his children,*
*and that is what we are!*
*—1 John 3:1*

# CONTENTS

# Dancing in the Aisle

❖ The Father's Legacy ❖

My father was my hero. The kindest, gentlest man I have ever known. The person in my life who was always the most like Jesus to me and consistently reflected the qualities of my Abba Father.

Before anyone in the music industry had ever heard my name, back when I was in middle school playing in garage bands in our hometown of Kenova, West Virginia, my father was always my biggest fan.

Even though he is in Heaven now, my dad, Paul Smith, is still my hero.

My father spent forty-plus years as a blue-collar worker at the Ashland Oil Refinery in Catlettsburg, Kentucky. Making the ten-minute drive twice a day, he crossed over the border between West Virginia and

Kentucky going to and from work. Even if he was sick, injured, or exhausted, all those years he was at his station working the swing shift. His work ethic and commitment to his coworkers were only surpassed by his love for his God and our family.

The memories of Dad's life, his words, and his wisdom are with me constantly as I parent and grandparent today. Between my mom, my sister, Kim, and her family, and my wife, Debbie, and our five adult children and all the grandkids, we have four generations living near one another. I'm so grateful to be part of a long line of love and godly legacy through the grace and mercy of Jesus in our family.

In his later years, Dad was diagnosed with dementia. He struggled with the disease for five years until his passing. During his first year or so in the battle, he would come to my concerts, sing at the top of his lungs, and dance in the aisle. *Yes, literally dance in the aisle to my music.* When he heard his son's music, a childlike quality came out in him during the season between the disease setting in and before he was homebound. Dad would introduce himself to the people seated around him and then ask, "You know who that is up there?" as he would go on to make the connection for them.

Looking into the front rows from the stage, the beam from my dad's countenance always appeared much brighter than the spotlight on me.

My dad went home to be with the Lord in November 2015. I miss him terribly. Grief certainly has no time constraints. But on a daily basis throughout his life, he gave me a glimpse of what God is like. Of course, as with all mortals, he had his faults. Yet the truth for me is that I just didn't see very many of them. You might suspect as his son I would say that, but *anyone* who knew Paul Smith in any of his circles throughout his life would tell you the same thing.

Soon after Dad's transition to Heaven, I knew I wanted one day to share all that his life taught me through telling stories from our journey as father and son, how he inspired and encouraged me, and how every day he quietly shaped who I have become. But alongside talking about the ways of my earthly father, I also have to share how our Father in Heaven has profoundly guided and molded my life, as well as Dad's, all of our days.

Here in these pages, I want to let you in on some lessons I learned from my dad and how those connect with truths I have come to believe about God, my Abba Father—principles and promises from the two most prominent and powerful influences in my life and ministry.

*Chapter One*

# That's My Son!

## ❧ The Father's Heart ❧

When I was growing up in Kenova, West Virginia, Dad coached me in baseball. No matter how I played, he thought I was the greatest. Even though I wasn't. One year, my Little League team played sixteen games with fifteen losses. As our season began that year, Dad made our team a deal: when we would win a game, we would all go to Dairy Queen—his treat. Well, even after the game where we got beat 30–0 and we were all hanging our heads in Little League shame as if our eight-year-old worlds had come crashing down, my dad walked into the dugout and said, "Boys, we'll get 'em next time. Now, let's go to Dairy Queen!"

Suddenly, striking out and cowering all the way back to the dugout or watching the ball somehow pass right over your glove to allow another home run was replaced by the sweet vision of a hot fudge sundae with the trademark curlicue top.

No matter the score or how poorly we played, my dad took us to Dairy Queen after *every* game. Often, because Kenova was such a small town, we would walk in the doors only to realize the team that just soundly beat us was already there, celebrating their domination on the diamond. We all knew what they were thinking and whispering to themselves: "What are you guys doing in here? We just annihilated you. Dairy Queen is reserved for winners!"

Those were the simple expressions of grace through demonstrations of kindness and generosity that my dad regularly did for others. They weren't the exception but the rule for him. On that Little League team, he gave every one of us young boys a constant reflection of how much God loved us. Our team always received what Dad chose to give us, rather than the focus being solely on how well we had performed in any game. It was as if my dad said to us with few words and a heart of action, "You might not feel like you deserve to be here. Maybe others say you shouldn't be here. But I'm the coach. I'm the father in charge. I say you can, so you will. It's about my provision, not your performance." This is reminiscent of the apostle Paul's words in Ephesians 2:8:

> God saved you by his grace when you believed. And you can't take credit for this; it is a gift from God.

I played baseball with Dad as my coach until I was fifteen years old. That last year, for the first time in all my years of playing, I didn't make the all-star team. But by that point, I knew that music was the new connecting thread in the fabric of my life. So, my dad turned in his glove and became my unofficial, unpaid, but always fiercely loyal PR agent. And even before I ever came to Nashville, he would brag about me and tell everybody how great I was, constantly telling me, "You're the best, son." And I would respond, "Well, yeah, but you're my dad. You're *supposed* to say that."

On one of my trips to the Grammy Awards when I was nominated, I didn't win. Afterwards, I called Dad from Los Angeles and said, "Hey, I didn't win the Grammy, but I want you to be okay with it because I'm okay with it." Dead silence on the other end of the phone. I asked, "Dad? Are you there?" He said, "Yes."

Then I realized he was mad. Not at me but at every single voting member of the National Academy of Recording Arts and Sciences that had decided to give the golden megaphone trophy to someone else. Finally, Dad responded with, "Man! What are those people smoking?!"

Together, Dad and Mom gained a reputation everywhere they went. They modeled the grace of God with a spiritual synergy only a lifelong couple who love Jesus can offer, but nothing in their lives caused that to come easily. Rather, it was by choice for them both.

When my mom was just eight years old, she and her three siblings were abandoned by my grandmother. My mother's mother walked out of the house with her suitcase in hand and *never* came back. Mom could have been angry about that abandonment for the rest of her life, but she chose instead to let God parent her. She chose better over bitter. And her life constantly reflected that truth, the decision to allow her Heavenly Father to take that role for the rest of her life.

My grandfather died suddenly of a heart attack when my dad was just sixteen years old. Dad was an only child, having had a brother who was stillborn. They had a funeral and chose a burial plot for the newborn they were never able to know. Tragedy and grief had deeply affected their family, and then at such a young age, when a kid desperately needs a father, Dad was responsible for a widowed mom.

Individually and together, my parents chose to put their faith in their Father and allow His strength and grace to carry them on their journey, every day of their lives.

Over the years—long after Mom and Dad had moved near my sister and me and our families in Franklin, outside of Nashville, Tennessee—I've become savvy to someone stalking me as I go to the store to run errands. I can feel strangers staring at me down the aisle, and then when I go to another aisle, here they come. Next aisle, same thing. Like a game of tag or hide and seek in Whole Foods.

Finally, I just let the person catch up to me to say something like, "You're Michael W. Smith, right?" I smile and answer, "Yes. Nice to meet you." But often, the next thing that would come out of the person's mouth was, "Oh, we just looooove your mom and dad." Those words have always brought a smile and a deep sense of gratitude to me. Not an autograph or a quick selfie in the produce department, but rather, "We love your parents." Amazing.

In our culture today, I am well aware that many people don't have my testimony of strong, godly parents. There was not a great father who reflected the image of God. Not even a good father. For some, no father at all. But part of the great news of the gospel is that God was the first and the ultimate Father, so He can father *you*. In fact, He *wants* to father you. He *longs* to father you. At any age and any stage of life, He is there, ready. Regardless of the presence or absence of your dad or your mom, God can be a Father to you.

> See how very much our Father loves us, for he calls us his children, and that is what we are! (1 John 3:1)

One day I was working on an album at my studio in Franklin. By that time, Dad was at the point of struggling daily with dementia. My mom called me frantically and said, "Son, your dad has fallen down, and I can't help him up! He's gone completely white, and I think we're going to lose him! I've called 911. Please get here as soon as you can!"

When I pulled up to their house, I saw a fire truck, an ambulance, and several other emergency vehicles, all out front with the lights flashing. I walked in to find Dad, just as Mom had described. I thought to myself, *This is it. He's gone. Dad's going to go to Heaven today.* Even though I knew he was ready and prepared, I wasn't. I just wasn't ready to let him go.

Finally, the paramedics got him onto the stretcher and wheeled him outside and into the ambulance. But then believing they didn't have time to get him to the hospital, they began to work on him right there in the back of the ambulance.

Now, my dad had all these personal sayings like, "What in the wide world of sports is going on here?" When he wanted everyone to be quiet and listen to him, he would say, "Hold the phone! Hold the phone!" While the paramedics were working to try to save Dad, I was standing and watching at the open back doors of the ambulance. All my parents' neighbors had come out and were standing around Mom and me. They all looked very concerned, and some were praying.

Within a few minutes, I saw Dad raise his head up just a bit. He slowly opened his eyes and saw me standing there. Suddenly, with increasing volume as he gained strength, he called out his infamous phrase, "Hold the phone. Hold the phone! HOLD THE PHONE!" Shocked by his sudden revival and outbursts, the paramedics stopped their chest compressions and backed up.

My dad then announced to those first responders and every neighbor gathered around, "Y'all know who that is out there? That's my son, Michael W. Smith!" I just smiled and thought to myself, *Oh Dad, you are just too much.* But his very first thought coming back into consciousness in this world was of me and his love for me as a father.

No matter who you are or your circumstances in life today, please know this—that very scene plays out in Heaven all the time as *your* Abba Father looks at you and says, "You know who that is right there? That's my child. That's my girl. That's my boy." His first thought is of you. And His love for you is that of a Father.

We can never step into our destiny until we know *who* we are. And who we are can only be determined by *Whose* we are. We can't get to that place of intimacy in our hearts with God until we receive the grace with which, as your Father, He lets you step into the winner's circle even when you lose. Even when your record is sixteen tries with fifteen losses. The only way to live from a strong place of faith is by accepting that knowledge, belief, and truth for yourself.

Regardless of who you are or who your parents are or were, regardless of their presence or absence, how good or horrible they might have been, I want to encourage you to wake up in the morning, look in the mirror, and find the strength in your heart to tell yourself, "I know I'm not there yet, but I like who I'm becoming." Why? Because of what Paul stated in Romans 8:10–11:

> And Christ lives within you, so even though your body will die because of sin, the Spirit gives you life because you have been made right with God. The Spirit of God, who raised Jesus from the dead, lives in you. And just as God raised Christ Jesus from the dead, he will give life to your mortal bodies by this same Spirit living within you.

I believe that to be true of you and for you. Together, we can confess with confidence, "Father, I love what you're doing. I know I've got a long way to go. I know I blew it yesterday. But today, I love who You are making and molding me to be, in *Your* image."

Unfortunately, the words "God loves you" have become somewhat of a cliché in our Western culture. But here's the other side of that thought that can change your life: you have to *let* God love you.

You have to receive His gift of grace into your life. Whatever your struggle, whatever your pain, whatever you have walked or crawled through, whatever you did to someone or someone did to you, God *can* father you. Just like my mom, just like my dad, let *Him* be your parent.

That has been my message since my dad went on to Heaven and as I have had the privilege of taking my music around the world. That is also my message in this book. I so want to deliver this simple truth that can set you free: God is a good, good Father. *Your* good, good Father.

> And I am certain that God, who began the good work within you, will continue his work until it is finally finished on the day when Christ Jesus returns. (Philippians 1:6)

*Chapter Two*

# Curveballs and Swing Shifts

❖ The Father's Excellence ❖

Over the years in interviews when answering questions about Dad, I have often referred to him as a perfectionist. But, like so many words today, *perfection* has taken on somewhat of a negative connotation by being attached to *demanding* or *stubborn*. So the more appropriate and accurate description of my dad would be that he was a man of excellence. The one person from whom he did demand perfection was himself. Yet I never recall him expecting perfection from Mom, me, or my sister, Kim.

His personal work ethic ran deep. His standards for anything he did in his life were high. But like so many from his generation, that expectation drove him to be great at whatever he did and whatever role he took on. That commitment to excellence was poured out in our church in his role as a deacon, and he often headed up pastor search committees and other critical layperson's roles for the church.

Dad stayed at his same position as a machine operator at the oil refinery from his hiring to retirement. I never knew the exact reason why, but he always turned down opportunities for promotions to foreman or any management position. I often wondered if it was because he knew it would take time away from our family, or if he didn't want to take on the stress that he saw his bosses had to endure. Or maybe both. But also, Dad didn't need any title to determine his identity. He was always clear on who he was and on his priorities: God first, family second, and then work.

The Pharisees asked Jesus, "Which is the most important commandment in the law of Moses?" His answer offered a blueprint for how to live and love: "'You must love the LORD your God with all your heart, all your soul, and all your mind.' This is the first and greatest commandment. A second is equally important: 'Love your neighbor as yourself'" (Matthew 22:36–39). The order is love God and love everyone else, but we tend to miss the *third* focus of our love and Jesus's last two words: "as yourself." Knowing who you are, accepting and living out whom God made you to be, is the catalyst for being able to love God and others. I truly believe Dad's endless drive to serve with excellence in everything he did with such joy was motivated by truths like these from Christ.

With the refinery running twenty-four hours, Dad always worked the swing shift, which meant for five days he would work morning to afternoon, then be off for two days. Then he would move to the afternoon to evening shift. Two days off. And then the night into early morning shift. Yet he never complained about the consistently inconsistent schedule. He just put in his time when he was scheduled to be there. He'd make the ten-minute drive from our house, work his shift, and in ten minutes be back home. Dad was able to leave the work at work.

There were many days when I watched my dad go to work in pain, sick, running a fever, or exhausted. But no matter what, he got up and went to work. In his generation, you had to be at death's door to call in sick. You just didn't do that. And for so many blue-collar workers, if you didn't work, you didn't get paid.

There's also the accountability issue that if you weren't there, the other guys had to cover your spot and work harder for the same pay. And for men like my dad, the last thing he would allow is putting a burden on anyone, especially his coworkers.

Growing up, Dad enjoyed carpentry and fixer-upper work, so for a side job to make extra money, there was a season when he built two houses from the ground up to sell. He did the majority of the work himself at night and on weekends. My sister, Kim, and I often went with him to help out in any way we could. When I got to put on my own tool belt, I felt so cool. Regardless of what we were qualified to do, Kim and I were free labor.

I can distinctly recall several times when my dad was finishing up a project on one of the houses, like a door jamb and the trim. He would step back, look it over up and down, tilt his face a little, look again, and then shake his head. Watching him, I would ask, "Dad, what's wrong? It looks great." He would say, "It's not square, son," or "It's off by a half an inch." I would try and talk him out of deconstruction with something like, "But Dad, no one is going to notice that being off by so little." But to no avail. He would take his hammer and a handheld crowbar and start tearing the trim off. Like I said, he just wouldn't settle for anything less than excellence with anything he did. To Dad, it didn't matter if anyone else would notice, because *he* knew, and the work had to be made right.

Because we both loved sports, specifically baseball, some of the greatest memories I have of time spent as a kid with Dad are him taking my sister and me on the three-hour drive to Cincinnati to see the Reds play ball at Crosley Field. And then in June 1970 when Riverfront Stadium opened, that ballpark became our favorite destination.

If you asked me how many games my dad took me to see over the years, I couldn't tell you because we went a lot. I lost count. One of the coolest things would be when, somehow, Dad would arrange for me to meet some of the team. I still have those pictures of me with my favorite Reds players.

In the mid-'70s we went to see "The Big Red Machine" every chance we got. Getting to watch the back-to-back 1975 and 1976 World Series champions was amazing—legends like Johnny Bench, Ken Griffey, Pete Rose, Joe Morgan, Tony Perez, George

Foster, César Gerónimo, and Dave Concepción. We both especially loved Pete. Dad respected his strong work ethic as a player.

I'll never forget that every time Pete was at bat and got a walk, he would run to first base. Not shuffle, not jog . . . *run*. Those early lessons from watching my dad and my sports heroes made a lasting impact on me as I began my music career. *Whatever you do, do it with excellence. If it's worth doing, do it well. Don't accept second-rate. Don't jog when you can run.*

Every time we came back home from those trips to watch the Reds play, I had a greater motivation and inspiration to play my own games better. I played short-stop and was a good ballplayer. Dad was my coach and taught me everything I learned about the game. The pro games we went to were like master classes for me.

America's pastime was such a huge part of my growing up and a common bond between Dad and me. For many years, as soon as he got home from work, we threw the ball on the front lawn. Him throwing from his left, me catching with my right, back and forth in a rhythm. While I was good at baseball, Dad was great at sports—period. He was a natural athlete and switched off between pitcher and first base. As a lefty, he would catch left, bat left, everything. So often left-handed players end up feeling like they have to change to right on some aspect of their game. Dad didn't. Somehow in my coaching, although I am right-handed, I learned to bat left. Some of my motivation was to be more like Dad in my playing. From my first year of Little League, he always told me there was an advantage in batting left because the pitchers had to adjust to you.

After I moved to Nashville and would come back home for the occasional weekend visit, I would stop in to get a Mountain Dew from a little corner store in Kenova. Every time I would go in, the store owner would start telling me stories about my dad's games. He told me again and again about times when my dad was the hero or how he would pitch multiple games in a row and win.

I would stand there at the counter listening intently as he would go on, like he was calling a play-by-play of one of Dad's games. The guy was good. I felt like I was listening to the Reds on the radio. Those moments were always fun for me and are such great memories today. It's amazing that a convenience store owner would want to make sure I knew that my dad was a stud ballplayer back in the day.

But here's the best part of my dad's baseball story: he was able to make it all the way to the minor leagues. His natural talent and skills were strong enough that the majors began to look like a very real possibility. But Dad was ultimately forced to make a hard call between pursuing a passion and facing a responsibility.

With my grandfather's death when Dad was just sixteen, my grandmother, Nanny as I called her, and his mom, was also now a widow. When my mom and dad got married at a young age, they moved in with my grandmother. The plan was for it to be for only a short time. But they never moved out. Dad made the tough decision between baseball as a potential career and supporting his wife and mother with something local and stable.

While we never discussed the subject, that may have been one of many reasons why he was so supportive of me pursuing music and then so proud when I began to get traction as a songwriter and artist. I was able to attain something he never had the chance to experience: taking a God-given talent and turning it into a career. There are a lot of similarities to a major leaguer out on the mound in front of a packed stadium and being at a piano and mic in a sold-out arena. Dad's past made getting to watch God bless my career from a front-row seat that much more special to him.

But I was doubly blessed because of Dad's character and commitment to family. I grew up having two moms in some ways. Nanny taught me how to play the piano. Well, I should say she *tried* to teach me. I always played by ear. Attempting to read piano music proved to be a little difficult. Nanny was the organist at the Presbyterian church in my hometown, so we always had an upright piano in our house for her to practice on. That piano and her encouragement laid the foundation for my transition from sports to music.

Following retirement, after Mom and Dad had lived in Franklin for a while, they decided to build a new home. Because of his experience with construction, almost every day he went to their lot and inspected the work being done on their house. While I know for certain my dad was always kind to any of the workers, I also know he had no qualms with letting them know if something wasn't quite right. I'm sure that builder was glad to finish up and hand my dad the keys!

By their later years, my parents had amassed a lot of great friends across the country. When I would release tour dates, my parents would look at the schedule and then a list of their friends. They would often match up people they knew with the cities where I would be playing.

The phone would ring in my manager's office, and Dad would ask for Chaz. The call usually went something like this:

**Dad:** "Chaz, we have some friends up where Michael is playing on August the third, and I was wanting to buy some tickets for them, and . . . if it's not too much trouble . . . maybe get them some backstage passes. But only if it's not an inconvenience."

**Chaz:** "Paul, I'm happy to take care of that, and we'll comp their tickets and get them passes."

**Dad:** "Oh no, I wasn't asking for free tickets."

**Chaz:** "But Paul, we get an allotment of comp tickets from the promoter for every night. It's okay. You're Michael's parents. If anyone can ask for these, it's you."

**Dad:** "But Michael or someone in his band might need them. We'll pay for our tickets."

**Chaz:** "Paul, we have plenty, and we're happy to take care of these folks for you! Now, how many passes do you need and what are their names?"

**Dad:** "Okay, well, only if it's not an imposition, or if Michael's not too busy . . ."

Chaz had that same conversation many times over the years with both of my parents. No expectations. No entitlement. No special treatment. Unassuming, with no desire to take advantage of anyone or their position of being my parents. Just like Dad not calling in sick when he had a fever, or not shrugging off a slightly crooked doorway on a house he was going to sell to someone in our hometown, or putting the knife to his dream of baseball for the sake of my mom and grandmother. That same drive for excellence and expression of work ethic caused him to try to pay his own way, even when he didn't have to.

But Mom and Dad were determined to show their gratitude for the free tickets one way or another. So randomly, unannounced, my parents would pull up to my management office in Franklin. Mom would walk in the front door with a freshly baked cake in hand, often still warm from the oven. But Dad never went in when Mom delivered those cakes. He would just sit in the car with the engine running, grinning from ear to ear as Chaz would look out and wave at him from the door.

Dad wanted Mom to have her moment in the spotlight on those thank-you deliveries. He just enjoyed being her driver as Mom was inside getting all the hugs, thank yous, and attention from Chaz, Greg, Derek, and the team. Taking the same back seat he took to me and everyone he loved to serve all his life, always in the spirit of humble excellence.

Scripture is filled with principles about the blessings from hard work and seeking excellence, while offering warnings against laziness, apathy, expectation, and entitlement. Yoking up the teachings in Proverbs, Jesus's teaching in the Gospels, and Paul's letters, there is a clear biblical mandate for us to do the right thing in the right way for the right reasons. Doing God's will in God's ways for God's purposes. There is an old saying that goes, "More is caught than taught." My dad certainly shared a lot of truth with me in his life, but far more of what I learned from him was from observing, watching, "catching" his tireless work ethic and constant desire for excellence in every area of his life.

Another amazing aspect of the gospel is that no matter the example any of us had growing up or our past personal history, our Abba Father can take us to a new place, teach us new truths, motivate us by His

Spirit, and place us on His path to a life of excellence. Every day is a new opportunity for a fresh start with an unending supply of His grace and mercy.

> Wise words bring many benefits,
>> and hard work brings rewards.
>> (Proverbs 12:14)

Work willingly at whatever you do, as though you were working for the Lord rather than for people. (Colossians 3:23)

You yourselves know that these hands of mine have supplied my own needs and the needs of my companions. In everything I did, I showed you that by this kind of hard work we must help the weak, remembering the words the Lord Jesus himself said: "It is more blessed to give than to receive." (Acts 20:34–35 NIV)

## Chapter Three

# The Marshall Plane Crash

#### ❖ The Father's Grace ❖

On a beautiful, crisp Friday afternoon in mid-November 2020, with the trees full of their vivid red and orange glory, I drove to my hometown of Kenova, West Virginia. Kenova is the last little town in the state before you reach the Kentucky and Ohio borders, about twenty minutes from Huntington, West Virginia. This trip afforded me a rare free afternoon to drive around and reminisce about my life growing up in small-town America.

Returning brought back so many memories of how sometimes after church on Sundays, Dad would treat our family by driving into "the city" for lunch. That was always a big deal for us. Huntington was also the home of Davidson's Record Store, where I would go to listen to the latest releases. I bought my very first 45 there by The Beatles that I still have to this day. I remember wearing out that vinyl when I got home, trying to pick out melodies like "Hey Jude" and "I Saw Her Standing There" on my grandmother's upright piano.

I had the time to stop by the church where our family had been members for years. As I slipped in and walked down the aisle of the sanctuary with the sun streaming through the stained-glass windows, I reminisced about singing with the New Generation Choir, led by our director and my dad's lifelong friend, Dan Ferguson. We had performed all the fresh, contemporary hymns that came out in the '70s, such as "Tell It Like It Is" by Ralph Carmichael, "Natural High" by Kurt Kaiser, and *anything* written by Andraé Crouch.

Dan was far ahead of his time in church music by incorporating songs from the very early days of contemporary Christian music. He brought in a full rhythm section of bass, drums, and guitar, along with piano. Dan was such a source of inspiration and encouragement for me in allowing the younger generation in the church to express our faith through modern music. No doubt that experience laid a firm foundation for me on my career path.

The experience of being back in Kenova by myself was surreal. Everywhere I looked triggered so many memories of my small-town upbringing. But the reason I had traveled here this time was not for nostalgia. I had been invited to sing at the on-campus memorial service at Marshall University, where the community would recognize the fifty-year anniversary of the entire football team perishing in a horrible plane crash. The news media would be out in full force for the event because the death toll of seventy-five victims is still the worst disaster in US sports history.

On November 14, 1970, the team's charter jet was returning from a 17–14 loss at East Carolina University on a dark, rainy night when the pilot got too low too soon as he began his descent toward the Tri-State Airport and clipped a stand of trees, crashing into a hillside. Thirty-six football players, five coaches, eight athletic department staff including the director, five crew members, and twenty-one members of the booster club, some of Huntington's most prominent citizens, were killed on impact.

I recall someone saying at the time, "For Huntington, the plane crash was like the Kennedy assassination; everyone remembers where they were and what they were doing when they heard the news." Businesses closed. Local government shut down. A memorial service was held in the football stadium. Because of the vast number of funerals, they were spread out over several weeks, which, of course, prolonged the grief and healing for the entire community. Because of the sheer impact and subsequent fire of the crash, six of the players' remains could not be positively identified, so they were buried together near the university. This was one of those events in life that, no matter how strong your faith might be, the enormity of the tragedy is difficult to understand and process.

The team had taken a bus to the game, but at some point, the decision had been made to charter a plane for the trip home. I also recall them saying that on the descent the aircraft was only ten feet too low. *Ten feet!* Only 120 inches made the difference between life and death, between an uneventful trip home and a horrible tragedy. Details like that cause so many thoughts of what-ifs for those left behind.

My dad and I were always major fans of the Marshall University Thundering Herd, and we often went to the home games. We had watched the game that day on TV, and my dad had heard that the team was flying back that night. When our phone rang and I saw the look on his face as he listened to the caller, I could tell that something was very wrong. When Dad hung up, he quietly said, "There's been a plane crash off Highway 75, right up the road." He grabbed his car keys and headed toward the door. At just thirteen years old, I stated, "I'm going with you."

We drove in silence through the rain until we reached a point where the highway was blocked by more fire trucks and emergency vehicles than I had ever witnessed in my young life. We pulled off the road to park, but at that point, still couldn't see the crash site. We could tell there was a lot of activity further up, so we got out of the car to walk. The rain continued to pour, and with no umbrella or rain gear, we quickly got soaked. But that was the last thing on our minds in the moment.

We walked about a hundred yards to the top of a hill, and then looking over, we saw the horrific crash with fires raging all over the hillside. To this day, that memory is so vivid and surreal to me, like watching a horror movie in real life. Even being so young, I still had the realization of so many promising young lives being lost in literally a heartbeat.

Standing there in shock for several minutes, with no idea how to fathom such a sight, and knowing we needed to stay out of the way of the emergency teams arriving, Dad turned and motioned for us to walk back. As we returned to our car, drenched from the rain, we sat in total silence. Dad saw a Kenova firefighter walking by, so he rolled down the window and called out to him, "Hey, was that the Marshall football team?" Somberly, the man answered, "Yes, we believe so."

With the confirmation, Dad's heart sank as did mine. The short drive back to our house that night was one of the few times I ever saw my dad get emotional. I could see the tears well up in his eyes and the pained look on his face. Dad was of that generation of men who felt they needed to always be tough. They just didn't talk about their emotions or feelings, negative or positive. (Anyone who knows me well knows I'm a crier; I have never had a problem expressing my emotions.) Yet on that particular night, Dad let me see his grief and sadness, probably because he just couldn't hold them in. The moment made a lasting impression on me. When you never see tears from your dad and then you finally realize he is fighting them back, you know the pain in his heart must be unbearable for him to allow the feelings to show.

I believe Dad was deeply moved that night not only out of his own grief, but for all the devastated families and an entire city that would suffer from such a tragic and sudden loss. The death of all those beloved players, coaches, and townspeople affected him deeply. I'm sure one of the thoughts that crossed his mind was knowing that so many mothers and fathers were going to be receiving a life-changing phone call that would break their hearts forever. The reality of witnessing that many deaths at one time, especially in the impact and the fire, was certainly more than my young mind and heart had ever had to process.

Yet in that moment of mutual grief and pain, Dad and I bonded in a way we never had before—a sadness both of us felt very deeply. I remember in the days that followed as the entire community suffered in pain from the loss, Dad was a great comfort to me, and I believe I was to him as well. Some of the strongest father-son moments we experienced were in silence, just an unspoken understanding of our mutual feelings, as if to say, "I get it. It's okay, and you don't have to say a word. Just feel what you need to feel."

Following high school graduation, not yet knowing exactly what I wanted to do, I went to Marshall for a semester and a half. With our family's connection to the school and the team, and also with Huntington being "the big city" that we went to for anything we needed that Kenova didn't have, I remember thinking, "Oh my gosh, I'm going to Marshall!" I loved my time on campus at the university. I loved my professors, especially my piano teacher. But there was one big roadblock I just couldn't seem to overcome: I didn't like my classes. Knowing music was my passion and life's calling, I entered the music program there. But singing operatic Italian songs while pop melodies were constantly running through my head just wasn't a good match for me.

After a heart-to-heart with my parents about my future, I checked out at mid-term of my second semester and eventually made my move to Nashville. Once again, my always-supportive father stood by me and believed in me, even though in that day dropping out of college to pursue a music career in Nashville sounded like an impossible dream to most people.

In 2006, when the film *We Are Marshall* was released in theaters, I wanted to go see it but was very concerned about how I would respond to watching the story play out on the screen. I finally decided to go, and at the beginning, when they showed the scene with the plane crash, I couldn't hold back my emotion. The tears came. I felt like I was reliving the moment of walking over the hill that night with my dad, seeing the fiery crash. I remember my wife, Debbie, holding my hand to comfort me. Finally, ten to fifteen minutes into the film, I was able to pull myself together. Seated on my other side, knowing my connection to the story, was Jeff Fisher, my good friend and the head coach at the time for the Tennessee Titans. I was grateful that the movie was very accurate to the story, not adding too much "Hollywood" to the actual events.

Still today, after all these many years, every time I go back to Kenova, I visit the crash site and the memorial on the hillside. I go there because of my connection to the community and the team, but also to that night when my father and I experienced shock and grief, and then hurting and healing, unlike any we had ever had before or since.

To close where I began this story, being at Marshall on the day they honored "the seventy-five" on the fifty-year memorial was such a privilege and a blessing for me, but also very emotional. I had to step back inside the building a couple of times to regain my composure. The event was held outdoors at the Memorial Fountain, where they had banners placed all around the plaza with the players' pictures. The fountain runs all year long, except once a year for a designated moment on the day of the tragedy, when they allow the waters to fall silent in remembrance.

Being asked to sing at the event and also share my experience of that night was a moment I will never forget. They asked me to sing "Amazing Grace," and then I closed with "Sovereign Over Us." *There is strength within the sorrow, there is beauty in our tears, and you meet us in our mourning, with a love that casts out fear. . . .* So powerful and so true.

Somehow in the emotion I saw on my dad's face that night, I understood for the first time, at just thirteen years old, that there will be moments in this life we are simply not going to be able to understand this side of Heaven. And that's okay.

> All praise to the God and Father of our Master, Jesus the Messiah! Father of all mercy!
>
> God of all healing counsel! He comes alongside us when we go through hard times, and before you know it, he brings us alongside someone else who is going through hard times so that we can be there for that person just as God was there for us. We have plenty of hard times that come from following the Messiah, but no more so than the good times of his healing comfort—we get a full measure of that, too.
>
> When we suffer for Jesus, it works out for your healing and salvation. If we are treated well, given a helping hand and encouraging word, that also works to your benefit, spurring you on, face forward, unflinching. Your hard times are also our hard times. When we see that you're just as willing to endure the hard times as to enjoy the good times, we know you're going to make it, no doubt about it. (2 Corinthians 1:3–7 MSG)

*Chapter Four*

# Who's That Girl?

## ‹‹ The Father's Faithfulness ››

I've spoken publicly on many occasions over the years, and will make reference in other places in this book, about that season in my life from seventeen to twenty-one years old. The bottom line is I got off track and became what Jesus called in Luke 15 a "prodigal son." In 1979, a year after moving to Nashville to pursue music, I finally came to the end of myself, had a complete melt-down, and fully surrendered to the Lordship of Christ. All my parents' prayers were answered, and I got a firm grasp on my identity and my calling. After working all kinds of odd jobs to pay the bills, I was offered my first publishing deal for songwriting in 1981.

On a Thursday in March of that year, when I was twenty-three years old, I had a meeting with Bob

MacKenzie, the president of Benson Records. At the time, I was 100 percent focused on my music. I was living, breathing, eating, and dreaming songwriting. Girls, dating, and especially marriage were *not* on my radar. With a new publishing deal, I spent at least four-teen hours a day trying to write the next hit song for a base salary of $200 a week. When those checks started landing in my mailbox, I thought I had finally hit the big time. In truth, for anyone trying to make it in the music industry, the transition from fitting your passion in between working odd jobs to making your living full time solely on music is a massive step.

As I sat in the waiting room of the third-floor lobby, waiting for Bob's secretary to call me in and reading the latest issue of *Billboard Magazine*, a girl walked by who caught my attention. As she disappeared around the corner, I attempted to go back to my article. But just as I started to regain focus, she walked by again, and I saw her eyes. In one strum of my heartstrings, I went from distracted to mesmerized. I thought to myself, *Oh my gosh! What . . . just . . . happened? Who just happened?* Something inside told me, *Smitty, your life is about to change.*

Now, let me be very clear. I thought this kind of thing would never—like, *never ever*—happen to me. I did not believe in love at first sight and would question anyone who said it happened to them. I would literally think, *How can that even be possible? To fall in love that fast?*

While my eyes went back to the magazine, I couldn't read the words because my head was spinning. I began to pray under my breath, *Please, God, let that girl walk by just one more time, a third time—three, just like the Trinity, okay? Please?* But then for a brief moment, my rational, practical side kicked in, and I thought about my music. *Maybe I should pray she doesn't walk by again?*

But God is good—all the time—and, suddenly, there she was. She walked right by me and down the steps toward the second floor. I threw the magazine down, stood up, and looked over the railing. I lost her on the staircase but could see the front doors and knew that she didn't go out. Realizing we were still in the same building, my heart began to speed up at a tempo just north of presto—two hundred beats per minute. (Musicians don't think in miles per hour.)

The only thing I could come up with to do in the moment was to go find an empty office and call my mom. *Yep, for real. Call my mom.* When she answered, I started to talk in a crazed frenzy, "Mom, you're not gonna believe this, but I just found my soulmate! I think I've found the girl I'm going to marry!" My mother, always a practical woman, asked me, "So, Michael, what's her name?" I swallowed hard and answered, "Well, I don't know. I haven't actually met her yet." (Cue Michael Bublé's hit song.) That was the point in the conversation when Mom began to get a little worried about me. She paused a moment and then said, "Okay, now calm down, Michael. Everything's going to be okay." That's when I decided to take action. I said, "Mom, I'll call you later. I have to go."

I headed downstairs and began to inquire with all the employees I could find, "I'm looking for a girl I saw a few minutes ago . . . brownish-blonde hair, about five-foot-three, small. She probably walked by here a few minutes ago." One lady smiled and said, "Oh yeah, that's Debbie Davis. Debbie works in the warehouse." So, off to the warehouse I went.

I walked in and looked around. No Debbie Davis in sight. I started asking the warehouse workers, "Can you tell me where Debbie is?" Someone said, "Yeah, I think she just went to the restroom." So, off to the ladies' room I went. But obviously, I waited outside for her. While standing there, I was excited that I had finally narrowed down the search from the entire building to knowing she was on the other side of that door. *Five minutes had passed since my last sighting, so what does it hurt to wait another two or three?*

Then sure enough, she walked out in an old t-shirt and jeans to find me grinning ear to ear at her. Like a good Southern gentleman, I held out my hand to properly introduce myself. "Hi, my name's Michael." She smiled, held out her hand, and said, "Um, hi, I'm Debbie Davis." I created some random small talk for a few minutes, but then unsure of where to take the conversation, I told her I needed to get back upstairs for my meeting. I closed with, "Great to meet you," and left.

Step one—meeting the girl—was now complete. *Check!*

After I was done at Benson, I had to go over to see Randy Cox at Paragon, the company that had signed me to a publishing deal. Benson and Paragon had just merged, so I was connecting with everyone.

In the meeting with Randy, I could not think straight. That conversation was a blur. No matter how hard I tried, I wasn't able to get Debbie off my mind. So when Randy and I were done, I drove back over to Benson and walked straight into the warehouse.

When I saw Debbie, I went right up to her and blurted out, "Hey, I wanted to see if you would go out with me. In fact, what are you doing tonight?" *Okay, I know what you're thinking, but as a twenty-three-year-old musician who just fell in love, my heart was officially running the show—and my mouth.*

Debbie very kindly answered, "Well, I'm actually going out tonight. I already have plans." Undeterred and determined, I continued, "Okay, well, what about next week? Would you go out with me next week? I'm going back home to West Virginia tomorrow to see my mom and dad, but I'll be back on Tuesday. How about next Tuesday night?" Debbie reluctantly answered, "Yeah. Okay. Next Tuesday," and we exchanged phone numbers (landlines in those days).

The next day when I got home to Kenova, all I could talk about was Debbie. I told Dad and Mom every detail about my new dream girl . . . well, all that I knew so far. Of course, the entire time my parents had to be thinking, *If you total up the time they talked, it might be fifteen minutes, twenty tops.* I can recall telling my dad that first night, "Because we're going to get married, you'll need to get used to her because she's really tiny." For some reason, I felt I needed to warn my dad that Debbie was small.

At home in Kenova that weekend, the hours trudged by as I tried to wait for Tuesday. Finally, I had endured all the waiting I could stand. I grabbed her phone number and called. When she answered, I said, "Hey, Debbie, this is Michael. I'm going to be coming back on Monday, a day early, so can we move up our date to Monday night?" She agreed. I had successfully narrowed the wait time.

I got back to Nashville on Monday afternoon, and we went out that evening. I splurged and took her to O'Charley's by Vanderbilt University. Afterwards, we walked over to Centennial Park and around the iconic replica of the Parthenon. We then drove over to Percy Warner Park, closer to her home. Sitting there in my car, I played her a cassette of my music. Debbie was the first to hear some of my early songs that would be recorded and released just a couple of years later.

At the end of that night, I wanted to see her again as soon as possible. I told her that I was going to be recording song demos at Tree Studio the following evening and that she was welcome to drop by and hang out. Thankfully, she showed up, and by the end of that night, I think we both began to sense God was up to something.

Soon after we started dating, I told Debbie, "You *have* to meet my mom and dad. Let's go to Kenova this weekend." I was so excited for them to get to know her.

When we arrived at the house, we walked to the front door, and, of course, they were watching out for us. When I reached for the door, suddenly it opened, and there stood Mom and Dad. They smiled, then looked puzzled, and asked, "Where's Debbie?" Being a bit shy about meeting them, she was standing—well, kind of hiding—behind me. She peeked around me and waved. As we walked into the house, Dad said, "My goodness, you're just a little thing!" (Remember how I had warned him about that right after I met Debbie? I knew he'd be surprised.) From that first visit, my dad loved Debbie like his second daughter.

With me obviously smitten from the first moment I saw Debbie, she eventually confessed to me that when she left the recording studio on that second night we were together, she cried all the way home because she realized she was falling in love with a musician. *Boom!* Now, of course, that statement calls for me to give you a little context on my wife and her life goals at the time.

Debbie is a native Nashvillian, a rarity these days since Music City has also become Transplant Central. She went to Wheaton College and graduated with a biology degree. She finished her education with a master's and was in the top three in her class. Following graduation, she came back home to Nashville to work full time and save money. Her life plan was to marry a doctor and go together to Africa to serve the poor. *That's* why she cried driving home that second night. I completely annihilated what she thought she was going to do for the rest of her life. But God certainly had a different plan for us than we were each thinking when we met.

As you might suspect from my pattern on day one in our relationship, Debbie and I got engaged three and a half weeks later. Yes, I said *weeks*. We set our wedding date for December. But then we moved it up to November. And then moved it up again and got married in September 1981.

Over the years, Dad would always say to me, "You know, son, you and I got something in common. We married well." Throughout our lives, even after my parents moved close to us in Franklin, there was never any weirdness with them being in-laws to Debbie. Just never happened. My parents were always a healthy example for us of a stable, solid, godly marriage. Dad provided a consistent male role model as a husband, father, father-in-law, and then grandfather and great-grandfather. Dad loved Debbie, and Debbie loved my dad. Well, honestly, Dad *adored* Debbie.

The role that parents play in their kids' marriages is so crucial, because there has to be such a sensitive balance of availability and support, all without getting in the way and interfering. Watching my parents provide that for us helped Debbie and I so much as our five kids began to marry. Their example gave us inspiration and encouragement in how to navigate our roles with our kids as they married and became parents themselves, along with the special relationships we developed with their spouses.

Today, every one of my kids will tell you that they had a front-row seat to a marriage that, for decades, grew in love and became stronger and deeper. My parents always showed affection for one another. If my dad left to go somewhere, he would go over and kiss Mom goodbye. When they walked, they held hands. The legacy that my parents passed to me and on to my kids is a 1 Corinthians 13 brand of love, lived out every day with no regrets. Debbie and I are grateful to carry on that biblical relationship for our grandkids and pray our children will live in the love God provides for two to not just *become* one, but to *stay* one.

> If I could speak all the languages of earth and of angels, but didn't love others, I would only be a noisy gong or a clanging cymbal. If I had the gift of prophecy, and if I understood all of God's secret plans and possessed all knowledge, and if I had such faith that I could move mountains, but didn't love others, I would be nothing. If I gave everything I have to the poor and even sacrificed my body, I could boast about it; but if I didn't love others, I would have gained nothing.
>
> Love is patient and kind. Love is not jealous or boastful or proud or rude. It does not demand its own way. It is not irritable, and it

keeps no record of being wronged. It does not rejoice about injustice but rejoices whenever the truth wins out. Love never gives up, never loses faith, is always hopeful, and endures through every circumstance.

Three things will last forever—faith, hope, and love—and the greatest of these is love. (1 Corinthians 13:1–7, 13)

*Chapter Five*

# Never Met a Stranger

## ‹‹ The Father's Invitation ››

Throughout my father's life, he cared for people. *Every*one. *Any*one. He never met a stranger, and he said "hello" to people everywhere he went. No one was so far above or below him that he couldn't or wouldn't care about them. My dad just loved people. My dad *saw* people. No one was invisible to him. The person mattered, no matter what. That selfless dynamic always stood out to me and challenged me to follow his example in my own life. To be intentional with people like Dad always was. To say yes to my own divine interruptions. To see everyone as God sees them—important to Him and His kingdom.

One summer when my parents, my sister, Kim, and I were returning home from a vacation in Myrtle

Beach, South Carolina, we passed three young guys walking down the highway. We immediately recognized them. They were each from families in Kenova. I knew them from school, even though they were older. Dad said there was no way we could just leave them on the highway so far from home. So he pulled over, turned around, and went back to talk to them. Soon, Kim was in the front seat between Dad and Mom, and all three guys were crammed into the back seat with me. Although we were tired and ready to get home, we dropped off each one of those guys back at their homes. Dad wasn't going to pass a neighbor in trouble and not help, whether next door or a hundred miles away on the side of the road.

Besides building a few houses on the side as I mentioned before, Dad also was an on-call handyman for a friend who owned some apartments in Kenova. Whether the middle of the night, weekends, or holidays, when someone had an issue arise in one of those units, this friend would call Dad. As soon as the phone would ring with the problem, he was up, dressed, and out the door to go take care of whatever happened. If there was some sort of crisis or emergency, like heat going out in the winter or a water leak that flooded out the tenants, Mom got involved too, taking food or pitching in however she could to help the family. What most of us deem as inconveniences to avoid, my dad and my mom considered opportunities to jump in and serve. Growing up with parents who responded to others' circumstances with such a servant attitude had a profound effect on my sister and me. Having traveled all over the world for so many years, I have learned to stay attentive to my own opportunities.

In 2019 I was booked to play in South Africa, so my entire team and I headed to Atlanta for our international flight. At the airport, the attentive lady at customs looked through my passport, then glanced up at me and declared, "Mr. Smith, you won't be going to Johannesburg today. I can't put you on this plane." Obviously taken aback and not aware that I might be on any no-flight lists as a potential international threat, I asked, "Uh, why not?" She calmly stated, "You don't have an empty page in your passport. South Africa is one of only two nations in the world that requires an empty page for their stamp. When you arrive, they will require that to let you in. Yours is full. No empty pages. If I let you go, you're going to be held in the South Africa customs office and likely sent right back here." Knowing all too well that these folks never joke and seeing she was dead serious, I responded, "Wow, well, I've never heard of *that* rule. So what do I do?"

We decided that my entire team would board the plane to South Africa, while the airline booked me a late flight the next day and a hotel room for that night. The goal was to give me time to get to a passport office in Atlanta to acquire some, as the customs agent called them, "empty pages."

Now, being honest here—years ago as a younger man, I would have gotten upset at my plans being disrupted and having to undergo some waiting game and bureaucratic chase. But I took a deep breath and remained calm. As I walked out of the Atlanta airport terminal, I whispered a prayer, "Okay, God, there's some purpose in this. You must have someone I'm supposed to meet here in Atlanta, someone I will encounter. I know You must have a reason for this happening . . . so, show me." But when you pray prayers like that, you then have a responsibility to watch and listen.

With my hotel several miles away, I had to call an Uber. Within a few minutes, one pulled up, and my driver introduced himself as Ruben. As we pulled away from the terminal, assuming I had just arrived in the city, Ruben asked, "So, what brings you to Atlanta?" I answered, "Well, I'm from Nashville, and I'm actually supposed to be on a plane to South Africa right now." He followed up with the obvious question, "So, why are you *not* on the plane to South Africa?" Ruben seemed like a sincere guy, so I told him the whole story about my maxed-out passport.

Obviously intrigued, he came back with, "That's crazy, man. So, what do you do?" I gave the short answer, "I'm a singer in pop and Christian music." Ruben then made an interesting connection. "I went to Bible camp as a kid," he said and then began to tell me some of his story. He talked about how he had gotten married and how his wife was "not into Jesus," so he then decided he really wasn't either. What became clear to me in that short drive was that Ruben had walked away from his faith.

But God was about to issue him an invitation back in.

I briefly shared some of my story of the prodigal season in my late teens and early adult years but how I had a radical encounter with Jesus that changed my entire life. Just as I said those words, we pulled up to the entrance of the hotel. Ruben put the car in park, turned back toward me, and with a determined tone, said, "All right, we've got about thirty seconds left in this car together. Would you please explain to me what you mean by 'a radical encounter with Jesus'?"

When I finished telling him what that meant in my life, he thought for a moment and then stated, "Well, two days ago I had a pastor in my car, and we ended up talking about Jesus. Today, you get in my car. There's obviously something going on here." I smiled and said, "Well, Ruben, I think you're right. There are no coincidences with God. I want you to know I'll pray for you. And I'll never forget this trip and you. I believe the Lord has a calling on your life, brother."

With obvious sincerity and intention, Ruben thanked me. We shook hands and said goodbye. As I got out of the car and walked into the hotel lobby, I whispered under my breath, "Well, God, that's why I missed my flight . . . it was Ruben." All the hassle and trouble will be worth it for this one guy. For an Uber driver in Atlanta who needed one more person to care enough to share the truth with him.

When crazy circumstances like my passport delay happen to any of us, as believers we need to look for what God might be doing. We can so easily miss it out of frustration or distraction. But it just might be

His divine interruptions, which He is allowed to bring into our lives, because if we call Him "Lord," He has that right. Just as anyone we love has the right to interrupt us for any reason, we must never forget that truth about our role in the gospel. We just have to watch, listen, embrace, and obey.

I could never have orchestrated a ten-minute talk with Ruben about his spiritual life. But God teed it up, and I only had to swing. He is in *all* the details of our lives every day and wants to do something in us, through us, and as an ever-present Father, with us. We simply have to pay attention when He interrupts our busy lives.

As for the rest of my story, early the next morning, I got to the passport office and, as you might expect, I ended up waiting awhile. Finally, when my name was called and they looked into my situation, I was informed that they would not be able to provide what I would need to leave for South Africa that day—a *new* book with clean pages.

Well, after many years of performing at so many functions at the White House and in Washington, DC, I have gotten to know some people in our government—past and present. I made a few calls, and, bottom line, having rarely asked for any favors, the office of a high-ranking government official immediately contacted the Atlanta office on my behalf. In our not-what-you-know-but-who-you-know world, within a few minutes, everything was suddenly taken care of, and I was given a brand-new passport and clearance to fly.

And that's how God chose to take care of me in Ruben's story. Just like I learned from my dad, when we follow in obedience, He always covers *all* the bases.

As everyone in my family and our team hoped and prayed, I was on a flight out to South Africa that evening. After fifteen hours in the air, when we landed and I walked into customs there, they had already been contacted by the US government to fast-track me through. To my surprise and relief, I was in and out of their process in record time with my first stamp in a new, clean passport.

Soon, I was out of the airport and whisked into a car with a police escort to the venue. An hour and a half later—and a long, hot shower—I was on stage in Pretoria singing about the sovereignty and grace of God. Something I had just experienced once again firsthand.

The older I get and the more like my dad I become, I find myself praying through the busyness and chaos of our culture, "Lord, please don't let me miss it. Don't let me miss You and what You have planned today. Help me be intentional with people, like Dad was, just as You desire me to be."

If you are a Christ-follower, the next time something or someone interrupts your life, fight back the frustration and negativity, and simply whisper, "Okay, Father, what are You doing, and what would You like me to do?"

Maybe you're like Ruben and need a gentle reminder that God loves you and will come after you to bring you home where you belong. Maybe this moment, in this book, on this page, is your divine *invitation* to come to the Father for the first time *or* the last time. I know from my own life, He is just going to keep sending His message of grace and love to you until you refuse Him or reach out.

Second Corinthians 6:2 states, "For God says, 'At just the right time, I heard you. On the day of salvation, I helped you.'" Indeed, the 'right time' is now. Today is the day of salvation." The great news and the beautiful point of this verse is that for thousands of years, yesterday is gone forever and tomorrow never comes, so "the day of salvation" is always "*today*."

> But in your hearts revere Christ as Lord. Always be prepared to give an answer to everyone who asks you to give the reason for the hope that you have. But do this with gentleness and respect. (1 Peter 3:15 NIV)

*Chapter Six*

# Loving on the Brokenhearted

❦ The Father's Rescue ❦

On the same trip to South Africa when I had the passport delay, I had concerts lined up in several cities. Any time I am invited to sing there, I try to make sure I have time to visit Living Hope, an amazing place I have been to several times over the years. Living Hope is a ministry that serves communities and settlements in Capri, Capricorn, Masiphumelele, Muizenberg, Mzamomhle, Ocean View, Overcome Heights, and Red Hill. Their vision and calling are clear and simple: to reach people for Christ, with the reality of what Peter called Jesus—a Living Hope—in chapter 1 of his first letter in the New Testament. Their ministry seeks to break the vicious cycle of poverty and disease in those developing areas of South Africa.

Living Hope's programs focus on education, social development, and assisting people in creating self-sustaining incomes. One of their major ministries, though, is the prevention, care, and treatment of HIV/AIDS and other related chronic illnesses that are so prevalent in some parts of Africa. Just like Jesus spent so much time healing and serving as a doorway to usher in and share the Kingdom of God, Living Hope continues to do His miraculous work in South Africa on a daily basis.

Unfortunately, on this particular tour, my schedule was not going to allow me to visit Living Hope. But God still connected me to their ministry one night in an incredible way. A few weeks after we got home, the director, John Thomas, called our office to share a miraculous story of God's salvation and deliverance, told in his beautiful and distinct South African accent.

John began by saying that he delayed calling to tell us because what happened was such a shock to everyone on their staff. He obviously also wanted to allow a little time to pass and be absolutely certain what they were seeing and experiencing was indeed real, much like what the early Christ-followers likely did when they heard about Saul's conversion to Paul. This was one of those stories that you pray will take place one day, yet when the miracle finally comes, you struggle to believe it's real. But that's when you *know* God is in the house and at work.

Unbeknownst to me, Living Hope brought a group of men to whom they had been ministering and caring for in the clinic's program to one of my concerts in Cape Town. John said that one of the men they brought could only be described as evil. John's intention was not to be judgmental or unkind in this description, but just to state the reality of what they experienced every day with him. (For this testimony, we'll call him Isaac.)

Isaac had reportedly killed someone when he was a child, and darkness had slowly swallowed up his life. Now, as an adult, because of his specific medical needs, he had come to Living Hope for help. Yet from a spiritual standpoint, no matter what they attempted, prayed for, and shared with him, nothing could seem to penetrate the stronghold on Isaac's life. He accepted their program and care but always turned a deaf ear to the gospel and had an aversion to any spiritual truth.

When Isaac agreed to come to my concert, their staff and the others in the program were surprised, and likely a bit suspicious, that he would agree to go to an openly Christian event. During my set, I looked over to my left, and with the lights from the stage spilling into the front row of the crowd, I saw this group of guys seated together. In the moment, I had a strong sense that these had to be men from Living Hope. Having not visited the ministry on that trip, of course, I didn't know any of the current patients in the program or their stories.

While sharing in between songs, I stopped, looked at the group, then felt compelled to focus in on this one specific guy. I very intentionally looked him in the eye and stated, in a totally directed yet spontaneous moment, "There is hope for *you* tonight." That man was Isaac.

As I started into my next song, I saw another man get up from a section further back and walk directly over to Isaac. Fully understanding he was a total stranger and taking a chance, the man cautiously knelt down and spoke gently, "I'm so sorry. I don't mean to be inappropriate or embarrass you or anything like that . . . but I believe God wants me to pray for you right now."

He then took Isaac's hands and prayed out loud. Like a Damascus Road moment, God's Spirit moved mightily, and Isaac responded in faith and was radically changed. John went on to say that since that night, Isaac had been pursuing God with all of his heart. Darkness had been replaced with light. His countenance changed from menacing and brooding to joyful and hopeful. Transformation came in an instant, and Isaac's hurting heart found a home.

I couldn't help but think about Isaac agreeing to come to my concert with the group and walking into a place where worship of *the* Living Hope would clearly fill the room. I wondered about him simply saying yes to an invitation to enter where Jesus would be present in power among a large group of believers. That reminded me of when Legion looked up from the tombs and his chains to see the Savior getting out of the boat.

> So they arrived at the other side of the lake, in the region of the Gerasenes. When Jesus climbed out of the boat, a man possessed by an evil spirit came out from the tombs to meet him. . . .

When Jesus was still some distance away, the man saw him, ran to meet him, and bowed low before him. (Mark 5:1–2, 6)

After Jesus delivered, rescued, and healed the man, look at his response:

As Jesus was getting into the boat, the man who had been demon possessed begged to go with him. But Jesus said, "No, go home to your family, and tell them everything the Lord has done for you and how merciful he has been." So the man started off to visit the Ten Towns of that region and began to proclaim the great things Jesus had done for him; and everyone was amazed at what he told them. (Mark 5:18–20)

While obviously Isaac's circumstances may not have been as dire as Legion's, the principle of him choosing to walk into the presence of Jesus and the end result being a radical salvation was the same. The bottom line is, even a small step of obedience toward Christ can change *everything* and *anything* in someone's life. John told us that everyone on their staff and in the program was amazed at Isaac's transformation, because he was clearly now "proclaiming the great things Jesus had done for him" to anyone who would listen.

A suffering man who had come to Living Hope for medical and physical help ended up meeting *the* Living Hope, Jesus, who offered him the cure he desperately needed for his soul. That trip to South Africa that got delayed from the start by a strange passport rule ended up being a mission where God performed miracles. I am grateful to have had a small role in Isaac's salvation, being able to see the fruit after Living Hope's staff had planted and watered for so long, and then witnessing the man in the audience respond to God's call to pray for Isaac and, in obedience, reap the harvest.

One of the reasons I love to visit ministries like Living Hope when I'm traveling for my music is from all the years that I watched my dad go every Monday night to a ministry that his church in Franklin hosted. Room in the Inn in downtown Nashville would load up a group of guys off the street and bus them down to the church where they would be fed, attend a service designed for them, and be offered clothing and personal items. They would spend the night in the gym, be fed breakfast the next morning, and then be bussed back to downtown Nashville. Dad was faithful to go love on those men *every* Monday night. Several times over the years I went and led worship for those services. I can still see and hear my dad walking up to one of those down-and-out men, smiling and saying, "Hey, ol' buddy," his common greeting for any man he hadn't officially met yet.

I know he walked into that group of suffering men each week praying to reach the Isaacs who would be there. The ones who showed up for a meal and a bed but ultimately needed eternal rescue and the Living Hope of salvation.

No matter what we do, retired oil refinery worker like my dad or an artist like myself, we each have a calling from God to live out. Between our moment of salvation from sin to the moment we pass into the presence of the Lord, what we all do for a living is vastly different, but our mission from God is the same. We are to share who He is and what He has done to bring light to those trapped in darkness and hope to the hopeless. We all have a story, and when we call Jesus Lord, that becomes *His* story for us, to share what only He can do to transform lives.

All praise to God, the Father of our Lord Jesus Christ. It is by his great mercy that we have been born again, because God raised Jesus Christ from the dead. Now we live with great expectation, and we have a priceless inheritance—an inheritance that is kept in heaven for you, pure and undefiled, beyond the reach of change and decay. And through your faith, God is protecting you by his power until you receive this salvation, which is ready to be revealed on the last day for all to see.

So be truly glad. There is wonderful joy ahead, even though you must endure many trials for a little while. These trials will show that your faith is genuine. It is being tested as fire tests and purifies gold—though your faith is far more precious than mere gold. So when your faith remains strong through many trials, it will bring you much praise and glory and honor on the day when Jesus Christ is revealed to the whole world. (1 Peter 1:3–7)

## Chapter Seven

# A Profound Presence

## ❮❮ The Father's Community ❯❯

When you talk to anyone in my family, especially any or all of my kids, everyone would say my dad had a profound presence about him. You could *feel* him in a room. You could walk into my parents' home, look over at his favorite chair, and there he would sit, smiling at you. You immediately got a sense of safety and security, simply because he was *there*.

In talking about her grandfather's presence, my niece Caroline shared, "My Grandaddy had a way of making you feel like you were the most important person in the room. I think his gift of intentionality created that feeling in you. He was intentional in *all* aspects of his life—his words, his actions, his work, and especially in his relationships. Nothing was ever surface level with him. That's why his presence left a lasting imprint on every person he touched, everywhere he went."

One of the great privileges of my career has been to meet thousands and thousands of people from all over the world and from all walks of life. But there is a very short list of those who, when walking into the room upon my first encounter, had a distinct, larger-than-life presence. A strange, almost mystical quality you cannot see but can certainly feel. Isn't it interesting that while we have trouble defining the concept of someone having presence, we all know what it means? Why? Because when we are in the *presence* of presence, we just know.

In July 2020 the world lost an amazing artist and incredible man, but for me, I had to say goodbye to a dear friend whom I deeply respected—Charlie Daniels. Charlie had become a legend *before* he died because of the life that he led. If you knew Charlie, you loved Charlie. At his memorial service, a man on his road crew shared a truth that I know from my personal experience: "Charlie was *never* inconvenienced by people." Never too busy, even when he was. He greeted everyone who interrupted him anywhere with a smile like they were an old friend. His attitude always communicated, "These are the people who have given me the life that I lead. If this is a particular person's only moment with me, I'm going to make it the best I can for them."

Charlie saw the best in everyone and always made the conversation all about the other person. *Every* single time I was with him, I would leave thinking the same thing: "I just want to be like Charlie." The big man with the white beard, cowboy hat, and fiddle bow loved God and loved everyone as "his neighbor."

Another example of an unforgettable presence was actually a couple—George H. W. (41) and Barbara Bush. Years ago, Debbie and I were privileged to be taken in by them as if we were family and treated like their own children. In 1989 I released a Christmas album and was invited to perform on the NBC TV production *Christmas in Washington*. Seated on the front row of the audience at the taping of the show were President and Mrs. Bush. When the show ended, a Secret Service agent walked up to Debbie and me and introduced himself. To our surprise, he then said, "The President and Mrs. Bush would like us to escort you both back to the White House for a reception with some of the other artists. Would you join them?" Of course, we agreed, and within minutes, we were riding with the Secret Service and pulling up to the White House. That was such a surreal moment for us.

At one point during the evening, Debbie was in a group with Mrs. Bush, listening to the First Lady tell stories as only she could with her classic wit and humor, while I was in the next room enthralled by the president talking about his trip abroad to visit with Gorbachev. Needless to say, we had no idea our evening in Washington, DC, would end like this.

As everyone gathered back together in the main room, the President asked if I would sit at the piano and lead the group in Christmas carols, which I gladly did. We were quite a caroling group, with Olivia Newton-John and Vic Damone standing by the piano and singing along. Later, as everyone was saying their goodbyes, the President told me he would invite Debbie and me back and would love to stay in touch. I thought he was just being a gracious host until several months later we received another invitation. That impromptu night began our friendship with the senior Bushes and eventually the entire Bush family.

I want to be clear that any time I talk about the Bushes and their legacy, it has *nothing* to do with politics for me; they were simply some of the sweetest, kindest, and most generous people I have ever known. Out of respect for the position, you always call past presidents by that title for the rest of their lives. So most of the time, I called him President Bush, just as later, I called his son the same. But on many occasions, I affectionately called George H. W. Bush "Number 41." Like Charlie, President Bush always placed the focus on the other person. Any time I was with him, before I would leave, he would tear up because he knew I was going to pray for him. And we both appreciated those moments together with faith as our common bond.

When I decided to establish Rocketown, the nonprofit youth outreach center we started in the mid-'90s located near downtown Nashville with the goal of being a place of peace, purpose, and possibilities for young people, President Bush (41) offered to take the lead in our fundraising. He knew my heart to rescue kids and believed he could help make the dream a reality. With his selfless efforts and leadership, we raised the money needed to fund the entire project. By 2019 Rocketown had over 18,000 youth visits and 250,000-plus community visits annually, representing every social demographic in the metro Nashville area.

I can't talk about people I have had the privilege of getting to know who exude a strong presence without bringing up someone who has come to be identified by the world with just one name: Bono from the iconic band U2. His humanitarian efforts, driven by his strong faith in Jesus Christ, have rivaled his reputation as the lead singer on chart-topping hits. I was first introduced to this anomaly in the rock music world in December 2002.

Bono was traveling throughout the US on a tour bus, speaking at churches and universities to bring awareness to the HIV/AIDS crisis in Africa with the goal of igniting a movement in the church to respond biblically. A friend of mine, Mark Rogers, called me and said, "Hey, Bono from U2 is coming to Nashville. He'll be at Charlie Peacock's house to talk to a group of artists, and I want you to be there." I was on a Christmas tour at the time but felt I needed to attend. After a concert, I flew back late so I could be at the meeting at Charlie's house the next morning.

As the eclectic group of Christian artists gathered around, just as you would suspect, Bono was passionate in his plea about the Western world taking action in Africa. He was asking the Body of Christ to step up.

I will never forget that at one point he picked up an acoustic guitar and began to sing, "We are one in the Spirit, we are one in the Lord." So powerful to communicate his heart in a simple, traditional worship song.

When the meeting was over, Mark and a few staff members were going to drive Bono to his next engagement in Nashville to meet with Bill Frist. Mark invited me to ride along. I think at the time Bono knew I was an artist but was not familiar with my music. Having come back home for one day from my tour just for this meeting, I agreed to go.

Out on the interstate, for the next twenty-five minutes, Bono spoke one on one with me with great passion and intentionality about his plan to establish what would become the ONE Campaign. He had heard that I knew the Bush family. We both agreed that I should at least make an effort to see if the president would agree to hear about Bono's vision. At the time, George W. Bush (43) was in his first term in office.

Fully grasping the desperation of the crisis in Africa and agreeing that the Body of Christ should alleviate suffering any time and anywhere we can, I decided the next time I visited with President Bush (43), I would bring up the subject. Our talks were never about politics or issues, but family and faith. Interestingly, when that visit came about, the president observed, "It seems like you have something on your mind." I simply answered, "Yes, I'd like to talk to you about Africa and the HIV/AIDS crisis there." I went on to tell him about Bono and the meeting in Nashville, as well as the van ride when he and I spoke directly.

President Bush (43) agreed to hear Bono's plan. I was not at all surprised that over the next few years the two became good friends, both utilizing their platforms to enact change. With a number of influential factors coming together, in 2003 the President created the PEPFAR Bill (President's Emergency Plan for AIDS Relief) to provide $15 billion dollars for cumulative funding for HIV/AIDS treatment, prevention, and research, making it the largest global health program to be focused on a single disease. The bill was updated and extended in 2008, 2013, and 2018 for an estimated cumulative total of $80 billion.

One of the great blessings and privileges of the platform that God has allowed me to have is being a "dot-connector" for Him, getting the people in the room that He wants for His purposes, to then do what only He can do. When you consider a random group of musicians meeting in Nashville ended up being a connecting point to the president of the United States and a global rock star from Ireland to change the lives of people in Africa, only God can take the credit for creating an outcome like that.

> Look around at the nations;
>> look and be amazed!
> For I am doing something in your own day,
>> something you wouldn't believe
>> even if someone told you about it.
>> (Habakkuk 1:5)

Another powerful presence in my life that made a consistent and eternal impact on me was Reverend Billy Graham. I had been invited by the Graham Association to perform for several events, but in 1994 Billy made a decision to change up his iconic crusades with a move that was deemed risky by many in the evangelical community, including some of his own staff members. On the Saturday night of his multi-day crusades, he would hold Youth Night. For that one night, he would change out George Beverly Shea, Cliff Barrows, and the traditional choir for me and DC Talk. He took out ads on the local MTV affiliate and pop radio stations. His vision was to reach teenagers and young adults that might not otherwise come to his event. The first night was at Cleveland Stadium in Ohio.

The result was a capacity crowd of close to 80,000. DC Talk went on first, and then I transitioned my set from my pop hits to worship to set the tone and get people ready to hear the gospel. Billy's message that night was one of the most powerful I ever heard him give. When he concluded and began the invitation, we all stood side-stage and watched 10,000 young people stream from all over the stadium to come down on the field to make a decision for Christ. I remember looking over at TobyMac, and we were both undone. We could not hold back the tears. Everyone on Billy's staff, including the ones who didn't think the event would work, were all in tears too.

Starting in 1994, I played at every Billy Graham Crusade, and, needless to say, they were all highlights of my career. In fact, I was at the very last one Reverend Graham did in New York City.

I will never forget after I had been booked for that first night in Cleveland, when I told my dad that I was going to get to do my music at a youth night for Billy

Graham. He was so excited for me to have that opportunity because, of course, Dad had such great respect and admiration for Reverend Graham.

Over the years when I had the opportunity to visit with Reverend Graham, always before I left, he prayed for me. In those moments, I sensed he was imparting something from the Lord to me. With him knowing the calling on my life in music, I had a strong feeling that he was spiritually fathering me. In his later years, when he was no longer going out to speak and his health was declining, I would go visit, sit at his piano, and sing hymns for him. I also had the blessing of returning the ministry and influence he had on me all those years when, before I left, I would pray for him—a surreal opportunity that I always saw as a humbling privilege.

Today, especially in our current culture, we cannot confuse *presence* with *celebrity*. Celebrity is a very separate concept. I have met lots of people who, only for a short-lived season or for many years, have been considered celebrities. These are people who have become famous for something, whether for their fifteen minutes or for decades of creating an art form. But celebrity does not necessarily equate with presence. Presence is something altogether distinct and different. A fascinating and intriguing reality is that I have experienced presence around people who are *not* famous and likely never will be.

My family has talked many times about the strange effect of walking into my parents' home those first few weeks after Dad went home to be with the Lord, instinctively looking over at his chair and missing his presence. More than an empty space, there was a huge void created by his absence. Not just someone we loved missing but a catalyst in our lives that was no longer there. Our eyes were all trained to walk in and look over for Dad, or Grandaddy, but his presence, his spirit was gone. When someone with that kind of presence is suddenly taken from you, there is a greater, deeper, tougher sense of loss to overcome.

The greatest display of presence the world has ever known came when a man, only around thirty years old, began to draw huge crowds on the hillside and talk about the Kingdom of God. The only authority the people knew in that day was government rulers and religious leaders. They didn't trust most of them and feared all of them, but this man was quite different. They could *sense* something was unique. There was an unusual presence like they had never experienced before.

> When Jesus had finished saying these things, the crowds were amazed at his teaching, for he taught with real authority—quite unlike their teachers of religious law. (Matthew 7:28–29)

Presence does not depend upon the size of someone's social media following, personal platform, or circles of influence. The more someone, anyone, allows the presence of Christ to manifest in his or her life—to love Him with all his or her heart, soul, and mind—the more of that same authoritative presence will be implanted in the person and experienced by others. The greatest men and women I have had the privilege of meeting were the ones who had the greatest level of surrender to Christ in their lives.

To our Abba Father, whether your name is Billy Graham or Paul Smith, the same opportunity and end result is there, to be saturated in the power and presence of the Holy Spirit. God alone gets to decide the size of our platform because He is all about quality, not quantity. Whether we are called to reach the world or our neighborhood, God determines and offers the size of the assignments. We are simply called to obey.

There is another type of presence that God offers. This is not one we contain within us, but rather one we give away. When I had any sort of crisis or problem arise in my life, of course I wanted to hear my dad's advice or receive his help, but the most important gift he offered me in those moments was simply this: his presence. Before Dad said a word or lifted a finger, just him being in the room with me or on the other end of the phone when I was on the road was so powerful. Someone sitting with you in the silence and just being *present* can make you feel like maybe, just maybe, everything is going to be all right, and that is a strong ministry.

When you aren't certain what to say to someone who just tragically lost a loved one, offer the ministry of presence. Words are going to fail. Quoted Scriptures can feel forced. So just be there with them. Presence cares.

When a friend calls to tell you that his or her spouse has left for good, whether you have personally ever experienced that level of betrayal or heartbreak or not, offer the ministry of presence. A hug, a hand-hold, tears shared. Presence listens.

When a coworker walks into your space and says he or she just got let go with no warning, be present. Whatever you know you would need in such a moment, do that, be that. Presence serves.

In today's culture, ignoring others' pain, looking the other way, working to not get involved, hoping someone else will help, or worse, criticizing the situation, is an epidemic at an all-time high. Compassion has become a dying art. God needs those who will be brave enough to offer *their* presence to be a vessel of *His* presence.

Unfortunately, just as I have experienced, earthly dads pass away, people leave, stuff happens, and life ends. There are going to be many circumstances we face where no one is available for us in the physical sense. Even in a crowd of people, we can feel alone, and nothing will seem to help. That is when the presence of God through His Holy Spirit can be with us— anytime, anywhere, in any and all situations. Nothing too small, nothing too big.

God is everywhere, but when we need Him, His presence can manifest in the room in a powerful and majestic way. Countless times, I have experienced His presence with me in my home but also on the other side of the world, in massive crowds and totally alone. God the Father is *always* present.

To solve the problem of sin, death, and Hell, Jesus came to earth. He became present in the flesh and in the Spirit. His sacrifice and resurrection now allow us to have His Spirit be present *in us*. No longer contained in the Holy of Holies in the Temple, we have become His temple where His Spirit dwells. That, my friend, gives you the ability to experience His presence and then to offer His ministry of presence.

In a 2016 article on PremierChristianity.com, Jon Foreman of Switchfoot commented with a deep honesty on the meeting with Bono at Charlie Peacocks's house, "I would not have dropped everything and booked a ticket at the last minute to hear a social worker discuss the problems in Africa. I am a selfish, star-struck, rich, American, Anglo-Saxon fan of Bono. He took a couple of hours to talk to a bunch of fans to tell them to use their clout to change the world. To feed the poor, to clothe the homeless, to heal the sick, to preach the good news of the kingdom of Heaven. Sounds like an odd headline: 'Bono Comes to Nashville to Convert the Christian Music Industry.' I was convicted. Guilty."

In every example I offered in this chapter—Charlie Daniels, the Bushes, Billy Graham, Bono, and my dad—the game-changing factor was not celebrity or power, but a selfless focus on others. Charlie's focus was always on anyone he encountered, gracious and generous, regardless of who they were. My experience with the Bush family was not about politics, but their desire to help people, whether street kids in Nashville or Africans dying of a horrible disease. Bono may have gotten on the world's radar by being a rock star, but he uses his position to do exactly what Jon Foreman stated for the glory of God. And then there was Billy Graham, the man the Father worked through to bring more people into the kingdom of God than anyone in history.

The one common thread in all these people is the single most important Presence on this earth—Jesus. And he told us in Matthew 25 where He will *always* be found.

> "Then the King will say to those on his right, 'Come, you who are blessed by my Father, inherit the Kingdom prepared for you from the creation of the world. For I was hungry,

and you fed me. I was thirsty, and you gave me a drink. I was a stranger, and you invited me into your home. I was naked, and you gave me clothing. I was sick, and you cared for me. I was in prison, and you visited me.'

"Then these righteous ones will reply, 'Lord, when did we ever see you hungry and feed you? Or thirsty and give you something to drink? Or a stranger and show you hospitality? Or naked and give you clothing? When did we ever see you sick or in prison and visit you?'

"And the King will say, 'I tell you the truth, when you did it to one of the least of these my brothers and sisters, you were doing it to me!'" (vv. 34–40)

*Chapter Eight*

# Go Get 'Em!

« The Father's Call »

In February 2013 we scheduled one of the most unique tours in my career. We started out in Sri Lanka at the Hevelock Sports Club Ground; then we went to Malaysia and played the Grace Convention Centre. From there, we traveled to Singapore to play at the Toa Payoh Methodist Church. But this story is actually about our last stop—the Bahrain International Circuit.

Internationally, there is a huge appetite for the classic worship songs that began in the Western Church and eventually spread to believers in other countries, most especially where there is any sort of aversion or even persecution of the Church. One positive aspect of the Internet and streaming services is access to worship music in places that previously couldn't get physical product like CDs.

For the Bahrain event, I was sponsored by a committee of just five people. But here's the incredibly unique aspect of this invitation: the team was made up of a Muslim, a Hindu, a Jew, a Catholic, and a Protestant. Their common bond, the stated goal, was a desire for peace in their nation and a call to de-escalate the constant tensions and volatility so well known in the Middle East. This group knew their vast spiritual differences and disagreements but set those aside to display a united front for advocating peace—something they could respectfully agree upon and work toward together. *Couldn't we all take a page from that book in this divisive age?*

The surreal part of this invitation was that to even be invited, my visit had to be approved by the king of Bahrain. He first became the monarch in 1999 and then in 2002 became king through the lineage of his family, the Al Khalifa dynasty, which has reigned in that nation since 1783. So, understanding the weight of such an opportunity, I felt like this was a God-thing and told my team, "I believe I'm *supposed* to go."

Our flight from Sri Lanka to Bahrain landed at around 2:30 in the morning, so of course we were all exhausted from the grueling international flights. Going through customs in Middle Eastern countries can be an incredibly intimidating experience, especially for a bunch of musicians from Nashville. As you can probably imagine, we were stared down while we waited for our entry into the country to be approved and to get our passports stamped. I'm sure we were an odd sight to them, especially by arriving in the middle of the night.

But we finally got through customs unscathed and felt we could breathe a bit easier as we walked into the airport lobby. There, we met about twenty people, all smiles, in matching shirts with my name emblazoned on them. They were so excited we had arrived in their country. When they led us outside to the vans that would take us to our hotel, I looked over to see this guy leaning against his truck. I was immediately alarmed. The best way I can describe him is that he looked a lot like the character that was Harrison Ford's sidekick in *Indiana Jones and the Last Crusade*.

While I tried to be cool on the outside, I was thinking, *Why is he standing there at three in the morning?*

*Why is he staring at us? Should I be concerned? Why isn't anyone else concerned?* My questions were suddenly interrupted when he began to sing very loudly in English in his awesome accent, "Aaahhhhleluia . . . Aaahhhleluuuuia . . . For the Lord God Almighty reigns!" Yes, the man began to belt out "Agnus Dei"! I did not see that coming!

I stopped in my tracks and turned to make sure that what I thought I was seeing and hearing was actually happening. I then walked over to him and reached out my hand. But he didn't respond. He just kept singing. Now, this was around the time that flash mobs had made another resurgence, and so, choreographed on the man's cue, around seventy-five people came out from behind their cars, all joining in as a mass choir to sing "Agnus Dei." I *really* did not see that coming!

Partly in shock, partly in awe—especially in Bahrain in the dark of night—my eyes filled with tears. I was so moved by the identification and expression of these obviously passionate believers. My entire band and crew were speechless. I think someone managed to get out a phone to record the moment. The organized gesture and welcome to their country were just unbelievable. It was one of those moments in my career I will certainly never forget and always be grateful to have experienced, one of my top five you-aren't-going-to-believe-this stories.

After shaking hands and thanking them all, we loaded up and headed to our hotel. When you get invited to an oil-rich nation by approval of the king, you get put up in a hotel that somehow even five stars just doesn't do justice for a rating. This particular one was off-the-chart posh.

The next day I went to a luncheon to meet with the five people on the committee, which bears reminding you one more time: a Muslim, Hindu, Jew, Catholic, and Protestant. We had a great time together, and I humbly and graciously thanked them for the blessing of being the artist chosen to have such an amazing opportunity. Needless to say, especially after meeting with them, I was super-excited about the concert.

Because of the potential for some people or organizations to oppose an event of this nature, the committee wanted to provide us with a seasoned security team. A large US naval base in Bahrain, with around ten thousand personnel, sent fifteen guys who had volunteered for the assignment, all believers and also fans of my music. (I never cease to be amazed at how my songs have reached around the world.) As I met each soldier, they were enthusiastic to offer us protection that we all, of course, hoped we wouldn't need. These guys were all highly trained and would stay with me, and around me, the entire day and evening of the concert.

But two hours before start time, the naval base began to receive intelligence reports of threats of protests and demonstrations at the event. To avoid any possible confrontation that might add to existing tensions, the naval command made the decision to call their team back. The committee immediately began working on bringing in a private security team. I had been told by the sponsors that this would be the first faith-based concert that Bahrain had *ever* had. That put an extra layer of protocol and protection on what was required and how to best proceed for such a historic event.

Like it was yesterday, I remember sitting in the hotel lobby, watching those guys leave, and beginning to get scared. In a Middle Eastern nation, you can't just take the attitude that threats aren't serious and that everything is gonna be okay. We've all seen the news reports of sudden violence, especially when there is so much anti-American sentiment in that part of the world.

My mind began playing scenes from the movie *Taken*, except all my Liam Neesons had just walked out the door! I pulled out my phone and called my wife. When she answered, at whatever crazy time it was back home, I told her what was going on. I ended with, "I'm scared, Deb." After a slight silent pause, in classic Debbie Smith fashion, she asked me a rhetorical question, "Michael, do you know how many people are praying for you?" Knowing she was right, I answered, "Yeah . . . yeah, I do."

Debbie continued to encourage me, "You're covered. Don't fear. People are praying. You are *so* covered by what is likely thousands of people who know *where* you are, *why* you are there, and *what* needs to happen." Her affirmation of the truth settled me down. My racing heart slowed its pace. I took a deep breath and let out a long exhale. The storm in my mind subsided, and calm was restored. I thanked her, and within a few minutes, a caravan of eight cars pulled up out front. Most of them were security personnel.

I was ushered into one of the middle vehicles, and we began the twenty-minute drive to the venue. To be honest, I kept looking out the tinted windows, thinking, *Who's going to pull up beside our car and start firing an automatic weapon? Or maybe a rocket launcher?* But when the entourage pulled up to the venue, there were no demonstrations. No protests. No one even holding up a sign. All clear. We walked into the Bahrain International Circuit, which looked like a basketball arena that was packed to capacity.

The committee had put together a choir from some of the area churches that came to join me on the worship songs. Throughout the entire concert, I was so moved by the passion of the people, along with the immense opportunity and impact that God was allowing us to have on this nation. As I led the crowd in worship, there were moments I had to try and hold back from weeping to get through the songs. At several points, I became so overwhelmed that I had to signal someone in my band to take the lead on the song. I kept having the realization that we were making history in the *middle* of the Middle East, on the infamous Persian Gulf. Together, led by an eclectic team of visionaries, we were ushering in God's Spirit to this country, for a specific reason, for such a time as this.

One thing I have learned over the years is that there is never an isolated event with God. Nothing is random. Everything counts. Everything matters. The devil is not in the details; God Almighty is! For Him to accomplish His purposes in a people, within a nation, He will often use worship to begin the breakthrough. So much has happened in the Middle East in recent years, and historic events continue to occur. God is at work in all those nations. That is exactly why, when the invitation came from Bahrain, approved by their king, I didn't have to pray asking if it was God's will for me to go.

I constantly pray for God to bring opportunities like this one, so for events such as that, the *invitation* is also the *answer*, the call from God. All He needs me to do is say yes. He takes care of the rest.

I remember when I told my dad that I was going to Sri Lanka, Singapore, Malaysia, and Bahrain, all places I had never been. Dad responded with a smile and a familiar, "Well, go get 'em, son." I know when Debbie reminded me that many were praying, my dad and mom were at the lead, so supportive, ever interceding. Like all good parents who love their kids at any age, they also told me, "Always be careful. Please be careful."

In 2 Chronicles 20, when Jehoshaphat was king of Judah, he was informed that the Moabites, Ammonites, and Meunites were coming to defeat them. Knowing the size of the threat, he became afraid, but he prayed and called on the people to ask God to move on their behalf. God answered.

Here's the story. (And just a quick geography reminder—this happened in the Middle East.)

Tomorrow, march out against them. You will find them coming up through the ascent of Ziz at the end of the valley that opens into the wilderness of Jeruel. But you will not even need to fight. Take your positions; then stand still and watch the LORD's victory. He is with you, O people of Judah and Jerusalem. Do not be afraid or discouraged. Go out against them tomorrow, for the LORD is with you!" . . .

Early the next morning the army of Judah went out into the wilderness of Tekoa. On the way Jehoshaphat stopped and said, "Listen to me, all you people of Judah and Jerusalem! Believe in the LORD your God, and you will be able to stand firm. Believe in his prophets, and you will succeed."

After consulting the people, the king appointed singers to walk ahead of the army, singing to the LORD and praising him for his holy splendor. This is what they sang:

"Give thanks to the LORD;
his faithful love endures forever!"

At the very moment they began to sing and give praise, the LORD caused the armies of Ammon, Moab, and Mount Seir to start fighting among themselves. . . .

They marched into Jerusalem to the music of harps, lyres, and trumpets, and they proceeded to the Temple of the LORD.

When all the surrounding kingdoms heard that the LORD himself had fought against the enemies of Israel, the fear of God came over them. So Jehoshaphat's kingdom was at peace, for his God had given him rest on every side. (2 Chronicles 20:16–17, 20–22, 28–30)

God still works in these dramatic ways as He moves in the lives of people. I'm so grateful to have been all around the world to see His work among so many, every tribe, nation, and tongue. You may never get called to places like Bahrain. But there are places and people where and to whom God *will* call you. There are people and places you can go, that you can reach, that I never will and never can. That is the beauty of the Body of Christ. And remember, sometimes the invitation is also His call. If we pray to be in His will, He will lead us to those places where we will "not even need to fight. Take your positions; then stand still and watch the Lord's victory. He is with you . . . Do not be afraid or discouraged. Go out . . . for the Lord is with you!" Just like my Dad did with me, I say to you now, "Go get 'em. You're prayed for. Just be careful."

*Chapter Nine*

# If There's Any Good in Me

<< The Father's Love >>

On my 2018 album release *A Million Lights*, the most personal song for me is "Footsteps." While the entire album is for my dad and is inspired by his life, that particular song focuses on my relationship with him as my earthly father. In a press interview when I talked about the song, I said, "If there's any good in me—other than God at work in my life—it's because of my dad." The lyrics to "Footsteps" offer a double meaning in my life because they are about my Father God, too. The beautiful truth for me is I can sing these words from the perspective of being a son to my dad and to Abba.

Maybe for you, when you hear the song, you wouldn't feel that you could honestly relate to the lyrics because of a lack of relationship with your dad. If that is you, then the great news—and one of the main points that I intend to play on repeat in these pages— is that this *is* true of your Heavenly Father's heart for you. You *can* follow in His footsteps. You *can* trust Him as your Guiding Light. He *will* show you the way. Because He *is* the Way.

When I was ten years old, while sitting in the back pew of the church with my buddies, the sermon one day was somehow different. Always being in church with my family, I had heard the gospel presented many times. This time, when my pastor finished his message, I had a massive revelation that Jesus was who He said He was. I had this strong sense of, *Oh my gosh! This is true!* When the invitation began, I got up and made my way past my friends as they all looked at me with a surprised "what-in-the-world-are-you-doing?" look.

I didn't just make a decision to follow Jesus. God revealed His truth to me that morning, even at that young age.

We know, dear brothers and sisters, that God loves you and has chosen you to be his own people. For when we brought you the Good News, it was not only with words but also with power, for the Holy Spirit gave you full assurance that what we said was true. (1 Thessalonians 1:4–5)

At fifteen years old, as I began to search for meaning and identity like most teenagers, one Sunday morning I got up the courage to walk down the aisle of my church. I quietly told our pastor, Stan Franklin, "I think music is supposed to be part of my life, like, for the rest of my life. But I don't know how to get there, how to do that. So, would you pray for me? Because I think that's where I'm headed." Being from a well-known family in a small town, everyone knew I was playing in little garage bands with other budding musicians, so the pastor prayed for God to show me my path to music, if that's what He had in mind for me.

As my passion for music grew and my opportunities to play locally increased, and as people in my church and the entire town of Kenova had the chance to hear me, they were so encouraging. People would often tell me, "You can do it! We believe in you!" When I began to mention a move to Nashville, everyone encouraged me to go chase my dream.

But at around seventeen years old, as hormones and angst and all the trappings of teenage life began to close in, temptation got the better of me. And honestly, just as God has a plan for every life, so does Satan. I know he did not want me to use my gift of creating music, especially for the Lord. The enemy will offer us anything to keep us off the path toward God.

As I've referenced in other places in this book, I became a prodigal son. But the difference between the young man in the parable and me is that I didn't go off to the far country with my inheritance. I stayed at home and rebelled. I went out and got into trouble and then came back home to my father's house. I didn't have to travel anywhere to fall into my father's arms. They were available to me any time day or night, and so were my Heavenly Father's. Even when I was away from my parents' house, God was always there, watching over me and waiting for me to come home to Him.

During those years my dad was, of course, disappointed in my choices and behavior, but he never expressed how he felt, never got angry with me or at me. There was never a moment of confrontation or condemnation. Part of Dad's motivation was that he wanted to avoid anything that might scare me away. He stayed concerned for me but turned his emotion into constant prayer.

Looking back, I'm very grateful that my dad didn't want to say or do anything that might cause me to leave and go to a worse place. Sadly, that happens all too often when the pain and frustration a parent feels causes a teenager or young adult to believe he or she has to leave. The desperation could lead down a bad road and to more poor choices. That said, the other side of this dilemma is there are times when parents are forced to make the call of enacting tough love. Sometimes a parent has to allow a child to hit bottom, and any sort of potential enablement has to stop.

A parent's decision on the best thing to do with a teen or adult child can be a tightrope walk with a lot of second-guessing and heartbreak either way. Each circumstance needs its own solution as to what is best for the person in trouble. As for me, at least being at home I was in a safe and secure spot. Kind of like a rebel living in a sanctuary.

Although I caused my father a great deal of sadness, he worked hard to be sensitive and try to understand what I was struggling to overcome. I remember once in that season, he asked me to come outside on the front porch and, calmly and with conviction, told me, "Michael, you need to stop doing this stuff. You're going to have to pull yourself together." In that moment, his words felt more like a warning from a wise friend than a threat from a disappointed dad. I was never given an "or else" ultimatum.

More than anything, Dad reminded me that I had a home with him and Mom. They just continued to love me in spite of all my really bad decisions. As for my own emotions, the farther I fell and the longer it went on, the worse my feelings grew that I had failed my dad, that I had let him down. I was constantly dealing with an overwhelming sense of guilt and shame from my own heart.

At the same time, the vicious cycle was that I also felt stuck. I couldn't find any method or motivation to pull myself out of the mess. That eventually became the really scary part for me. You can try and will yourself all you want and declare, "I'm going to just pick myself up, get my act together, and turn my heart back toward the Lord." But I could not find the strength to do that on my own. I was going full speed down the road and couldn't seem to find an exit ramp.

An internal battle begins, where we plainly know the truth and we can know the Father is waiting with open arms, yet we stay stuck or stray or walk off and go our own way. In Romans 7, the apostle Paul provided us with a brutally honest and vulnerable look at his own frustrations with this systemic human dilemma.

So the trouble is not with the law, for it is spiritual and good. The trouble is with me, for I am all too human, a slave to sin. I don't really understand myself, for I want to do what is right, but I don't do it. Instead, I do what I hate. But if I know that what I am doing is wrong, this shows that I agree that the law is good. So I am not the one doing wrong; it is sin living in me that does it.

And I know that nothing good lives in me, that is, in my sinful nature. I want to do what is right, but I can't. I want to do what is good, but I don't. I don't want to do what is wrong, but I do it anyway. But if I do what I don't want to do, I am not really the one doing wrong; it is sin living in me that does it.

I have discovered this principle of life—that when I want to do what is right, I inevitably do what is wrong. I love God's law with all my heart. But there is another power within me that is at war with my mind. This power makes me a slave to the sin that is still within me. Oh, what a miserable person I am! Who will free me from this life that is dominated by sin and death? Thank God! The answer is in Jesus Christ our Lord. (vv. 14–25)

I love that Paul gave an amazing description of the problem but then closed with the only solution—Jesus Christ. The reality for me was, yes, of course, my dad loved me and did all he could. As great as Dad was, though, he was never going to be my answer to change the course of my life. He knew my solution was Jesus, and that's why he prayed constantly for me to return to Christ, so He could not only be my Savior, but my Lord. One of the reasons I have spent many years creating worship music is because I have experienced the One who, as Paul said, freed me from this life that is dominated by sin and death. The sense that *I cannot thank Him enough* produces personal worship.

Maybe you are in a great place today and have never felt stronger in your life. Be grateful, and at the same time, be careful. Express gratitude for God's blessings, but ask Him to keep you from temptation and provide the way of escape that He promises will come when the enemy tries to take you down.

> If you think you are standing strong, be careful not to fall. The temptations in your life are no different from what others experience. And God is faithful. He will not allow the temptation to be more than you can stand. When you are tempted, he will show you a way out so that you can endure. (1 Corinthians 10:12–13)

Perhaps you are doing your best to walk with the Lord, but you feel stagnant and stuck in your faith. I get it. We all walk through seasons of drought when our faith feels as though it is in a rut. I want to encourage you to keep praying, stay in the Word, and watch for God to work. This season will pass, and your faith will be vibrant once again. Your obedience will meet God's faithfulness.

But those who live to please the Spirit will harvest everlasting life from the Spirit. So let's not get tired of doing what is good. At just the right time we will reap a harvest of blessing if we don't give up. Therefore, whenever we have the opportunity, we should do good to everyone. (Galatians 6:8–10)

Here's a tough one. Maybe you are a parent of a rebellious child, a prodigal son or daughter—from a preteen with an attitude, trying to push away any authority, to an adult child who has turned his or her back on God altogether, or any situation in between. I know what my dad would tell you right now: Be an extension of God's grace. Never stop praying. Don't let up on your unconditional love. Express care and compassion, not condemnation and anger. Even when you're 99 percent of the way to your miracle, keep praying. Press on. Stay strong. Your child needs you now more than ever. Love and pray like your child's life depends on it, because it just might.

Don't burn out; keep yourselves fueled and aflame. Be alert servants of the Master,

cheerfully expectant. Don't quit in hard times;
pray all the harder. (Romans 12:11–12 MSG)

Lastly, if you are in the state that I was in for a
few years—feeling miserable, stuck in a lifestyle going
nowhere, or in a downward spiral, here's my advice:
Don't keep trying. Just give up. Simply surrender. Tell
God you are done trying life your way and are ready
to walk in His footsteps. I would never tell you that
such a choice is simple or easy, but I can say this with
all certainty: I have regrets from choices I made when I
was not following Christ. But ever since I chose to follow Him, while, yes, I have messed up and made some
wrong choices, I have never once regretted the decision
I made to surrender my life to Jesus. And you won't
either. Let go. Fall into the Father's arms right now.
I know from personal experience, He is there. Our
Abba Father will never leave you or abandon you. He
is waiting at the end of the road for you to come home.
He will forgive and celebrate your return to Him.

I want to invite you to find my song "Footsteps,"
however you access your music. Take a few minutes
alone without distraction, take in the lyrics, and let
them encourage you today. But also be sure to listen

closely to the voice of your Abba Father as He invites you to follow Him, to walk in His footsteps.

> So Jesus told them this story: "If a man has a hundred sheep and one of them gets lost, what will he do? Won't he leave the ninety-nine others in the wilderness and go to search for the one that is lost until he finds it? And when he has found it, he will joyfully carry it home on his shoulders. When he arrives, he will call together his friends and neighbors, saying, 'Rejoice with me because I have found my lost sheep.' In the same way, there is more joy in heaven over one lost sinner who repents and returns to God than over ninety-nine others who are righteous and haven't strayed away! (Luke 15:3–7)

*Chapter Ten*

# Walking Down This Dusty Road

❧ The Father's Strength ❧

After over forty years on swing shifts at the oil refinery, Dad finally had to take early retirement on disability. Ironically, after that long working at what can be a very hazardous place doing hard manual labor, the disability wasn't in any way related to his career.

While in his mid-twenties, a group of guys that had all played high school football together decided to hold an alumni game—with helmets, pads, and full contact. *Typical young men thinking they are bulletproof.* During the game, Dad took a hard hit and collapsed on the ground. Seeing he was badly hurt and in a lot of pain, the guys finally managed to get him onto a stretcher. For some reason, no one called an ambulance. Instead, they put him in the back seat of Grandaddy Spradlin's car, my mom's dad, and drove him to the emergency room.

Following X-rays, the doctors told Dad that his neck was fractured and he had come very close to being paralyzed. He spent two weeks in the hospital and the next six months in a full neck brace. Over the years, he had multiple surgeries and even had metal rods implanted in his back in an effort to alleviate the chronic pain. With modern technology making so many advances in recent years, some of these methods have long been abandoned for good reason.

Everyone in our family always knew that Dad was likely in pain on some level, having good days and bad days. Unfortunately, living in chronic discomfort had become a constant in his life. To this day, my five kids talk about being amazed at knowing the pain he was obviously in, yet how he never let on or complained because he never wanted the focus on him.

They're right; Dad *never* complained. About anything. His glass was always half-full, in the process of being filled up, or running over! He never became reliant on pain medications either. The primary reason was that his father had been an alcoholic. Growing up, watching and being aware of his father's constant battle with addiction, my dad vowed he would never touch alcohol or any substance that might take him down the same road. Even after he and his buddies became legal to drink, Dad would hang out with them but always be their designated driver.

I believe the only thing that got him through the countless tough days of physical pain was his faith in the Lord, daily asking for and relying on God's strength and grace to sustain him. That was likely also a factor that drove his desire to serve others. He wanted to keep his focus on others who had potentially greater struggles. This was the same mindset that motivated Helen Keller's famous quote, "I cried because I had no shoes until I met a man who had no feet."

Dad's daily battle with pain often reminded me of another Paul, the apostle Paul, and his "thorn in the flesh." We never knew to what issue Paul was specifically referring in that passage, but he came to the conclusion that God had chosen not to heal him for his own continual reliance on the Lord and the greater glory for the Kingdom. This is a powerful reminder and encouragement for when any of us must endure a constant struggle of any kind.

I will boast only about my weaknesses. If I wanted to boast, I would be no fool in doing so, because I would be telling the truth. But I won't do it, because I don't want anyone to give me credit beyond what they can see in my life or hear in my message, even though I have received such wonderful revelations from God. So to keep me from becoming proud, I was given a thorn in my flesh, a messenger from Satan to torment me and keep me from becoming proud.

Three different times I begged the Lord to take it away. Each time he said, "My grace is all you need. My power works best in weakness." So now I am glad to boast about my weaknesses, so that the power of Christ can work through me. That's why I take pleasure in my weaknesses, and in the insults, hardships, persecutions, and troubles that I suffer for Christ. For when I am weak, then I am strong. (2 Corinthians 12:5–10)

This is one of the many paradoxes in the gospel—when we are weak, we can be strong, because He is strong in us.

For ongoing battles in the physical, mental, or emotional realm of life, taking on such a mindset and attitude reflects great spiritual maturity. When our Abba Father doesn't answer our prayers for healing the way we think He should, for ourselves or a loved one, the temptation often comes to question His goodness, to doubt His love and care for us. But one of the reasons Paul's deeply personal dilemma is shared in the New Testament has to be to show us that God will do what is best for us and ultimately bring us to the end goal of becoming like Christ.

We have to keep reminding ourselves, especially in Western Christianity, that God's goal for us is *holiness*, which doesn't always translate into *happiness*. Happiness is temporary, while holiness attained is permanent. While true for the Christ-follower, that is a hard truth to accept for us all. For our family, we watched my dad allow God to make him more like Jesus, when, of course, he would have loved to be healed of his back and neck pain. Yet part of my dad's testimony and legacy today is what it is *because* of the pain and his personal "thorn." Holiness won out over happiness.

A few years after I moved to Nashville, my sister, Kim, decided to make her home here too. Obviously, my parents began to visit regularly, especially after Debbie and I, along with Kim and her husband, started having kids. Dad and Mom quickly fell in love with Middle Tennessee. Following Dad's retirement, ready to be involved in their family's day-to-day lives, they sold their home in Kenova and bought a condo near us, eventually building a home here, as I mentioned earlier. Dad spent the next twenty-two years in our community, serving people just like he always had, even as he aged and the pain grew worse.

After Dad passed, my immense feelings of loss, grief, and mourning found an outlet in my songs. I thank God for the gift of being able to use melody and rhyme to express the good and the grief in this world that hopefully can also encourage others in their own journey. One of those songs was written with the brilliant Cindy Morgan, a trusted writer I have worked with many times.

With the song "Dusty Road," I wanted to communicate my dad's spirit of endurance, perseverance, and always moving forward to see what God had next, all in the context of those roads he walked and drove every day in West Virginia. I wanted to capture the essence of the many tough days that he went to work, whether the day, night, or graveyard shift, to do the same thing with the same men but to press into what the Lord had in store. To discover the majesty in the mundane, the grace in the grit, the compelling in the common.

In our current celebrity-driven culture, where social media demands us to display perfection to the world, there is a simple and honest beauty found in the lives of the men and women who became known as the Silent Generation. The name itself denotes how they worked tirelessly, took care of their families, and just kept walking down life's road, no matter how tough the journey became.

With my dad as the inspiration, here are the lyrics Cindy and I wrote. Depending on your age, you just might find your own parents or someone you love in your family in this story, too.

Dusty road, buried dreams
Pieces on the ground
Saw the ghosts of empty streets
Of that West Virginia town
He worked for years on swing shift
At the oil refinery
You loved your wife and your kids
And one of those kids was me

And the sweat upon your brow
Was like the tears of Heaven pouring out
You said, "Keep walking on down, down this
dusty road"
"We're gonna make it somehow"

Now I wish that you were here
You'd be amazed to see
That today looks like a page
Torn from 1933
In my dreams to you I run
In golden fields where angels kiss the sun
You say, "Keep walking on down, down this
dusty road"
"We're gonna make it somehow"

When I feel it, feel it in my bones
That there's a place up ahead that looks like
    home
We keep walking on down, down this dusty
    road
We're gonna make it somehow
Gonna make it somehow
Yes, we are

And a peace comes to me now
Like a steady hand to lead us out
Keep walking on down, down this dusty road
Gonna make it somehow
I can feel it, feel it in my bones
That there's a place up ahead that looks like
    home
We keep walking on down, down this dusty
    road
We're gonna make it somehow
Gonna make it somehow
Yes, we are.

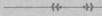

Living in a fallen world, the likelihood of having a thorn come into your life is not a matter of *if* but *when*. Whatever your pain may be today, whether chronic or new, physical or emotional, I want to encourage you to seek the perspective that the apostle Paul and my dad Paul chose to take. Pray always for God's intervention, but also allow Him to use the circumstances to shape you into the image of Jesus. For the Christ-follower, the best is always yet to come, because even when life gets hard to handle, Heaven is on the way.

Therefore, since we have been made right in God's sight by faith, we have peace with God because of what Jesus Christ our Lord has done for us. Because of our faith, Christ has brought us into this place of undeserved privilege where we now stand, and we confidently and joyfully look forward to sharing God's glory.

We can rejoice, too, when we run into problems and trials, for we know that they help us develop endurance. And endurance develops strength of character, and character strengthens our confident hope of salvation. And this hope will not lead to disappointment. For we know how dearly God loves us, because he has given us the Holy Spirit to fill our hearts with his love. (Romans 5:1–5)

## Chapter Eleven

# Not an Event, but an Experience

## ❖ The Father's Righteousness ❖

In the season following Dad's passing, along with my sister and our families, my focus moved fully to my mom and making sure she was taken care of and doing well. We all had to make the necessary adjustments. Everyone in our family had to find the "new normal," as they say.

After life had settled down a bit, I began to try to go back to my studio to write. Day after day, I tried, but nothing would come.

Over the years, I have learned that if I sit at the piano or play my guitar and, if after I make a solid effort for a while, there is just no inspiration and nothing jumps out as a potential song, I just need to call it a day and move on to other things. Sitting there for hours trying to force creativity has never worked for me.

Of course, as a songwriter, I have had many seasons of artistic drought, of varying lengths, when new music seems to refuse to be born. You might think that when that happens, the years I've spent doing this would allow me to cut myself some slack and not panic. It's so easy every time to think, *But I bet this time is going to be different.*

Well, the longer this particular dry spell went on, the more panic crept in. I even went so far as to think, *Well, God, thank You. It's been a great thirty-plus years. I guess we're moving on to something else now.*

I met with my team and shared honestly about what was happening, how I felt, and that I had accepted the fact I might not create for a while. I had no choice but to back off and wait. And pray.

About a month after that meeting, I went back to writing, but the creativity was coming very slowly. The way the Holy Spirit works is always fascinating as well as surprising to me. One of those aspects is in the way you can read a chapter or a passage in Scripture many times over many years, and then suddenly, one day you feel like you see its truth for the very first time.

That's exactly what happened to me one day during this season when I was doing my daily Bible reading and got to Amos 5 in *The Message* Bible.

The chapter is long and filled with God's statements of anger and frustration with His people. But as I got to verses 21 through 24—nearly the end of the chapter—I felt like I had suddenly been thrown back against the wall. My knees buckled. My breath was taken away. The words hit home and commanded my full attention.

> "I can't stand your religious meetings. I'm fed up with your conferences and conventions. I want nothing to do with your religion projects, your pretentious slogans and goals. I'm sick of your fund-raising schemes, your public relations and image making. I've had all I can take of your noisy ego-music. When was the last time you sang to me? Do you know what I want? I want justice—oceans of it. I want fairness—rivers of it. That's what I want. That's all I want."

The end of the chapter has a sort of signature, like on a letter or email, that reads, "God's Message, God-of-the-Angel-Armies." The chapter is titled "All Show,

No Substance," and that specific section is labeled as "Time to Face Hard Reality, Not Fantasy."

As I read the words over and over, I could envision God with His hands cupped over His ears, saying, "Stop it! Stop the music! I can't take any more!" Now, as you know, I'm a musician, a singer, an artist who writes songs for and leads music at "religious meetings, conferences, and conventions." I have a publicist. I have people that work to get my "image" out to the masses. And "your noisy ego-music"? Wow! Calling music "noise" and inferring ego is attached are some of the worst accusations for an artist.

I immediately began to personalize the words and ask, "God, have I missed it? Have I missed *You*?" I placed *everything* on the table and started reexamining my career and my calling. I laid this passage over my life and asked God how He wanted to line it up.

As a good and gracious Father, He began to show me His truth, just as Hebrews 12:6 tells us, "The Lord disciplines those he loves." In Amos 5, He helped me discover what my response should be to the current culture and what He desired from my personal life and my platform as an artist: "I want oceans of justice and rivers of fairness."

I began to explore these topics by reading the other Old Testament prophets, wanting to understand what truly gets God's attention. In my study, He revealed to me that *worship* goes hand in hand with *justice*. There is an obedience, an action, an expression that connects to the outward display of praise: taking care of widows and orphans, investing the time and energy to assist people who have fallen down and help get them "out of the ditch." Those sorts of acts of obedience *are* worship. For God, they *are* connected. They *must* be connected.

Another chapter that jumped out at me was Isaiah 58, where God told Israel, essentially, that they had Him all wrong. But it's so ironic and interesting how His words to the nation are so timely and relevant to us in Western culture today. God started out with this in verse 2:

> They come to the Temple every day
>     and seem delighted to learn all about me.
> They act like a righteous nation
>     that would never abandon the laws of
>         its God.
> They ask me to take action on their behalf,
>     pretending they want to be near me.

Then He moved to the correction in verses 6 and 7:

"No, this is the kind of fasting I want:
Free those who are wrongly imprisoned;
    lighten the burden of those who work
        for you.
Let the oppressed go free,
    and remove the chains that bind people.
Share your food with the hungry,
    and give shelter to the homeless.
Give clothes to those who need them,
    and do not hide from relatives who need
        your help."

And finally, He promises this in verses 8 and 9:

"Then your salvation will come like the dawn,
    and your wounds will quickly heal.
Your godliness will lead you forward,
    and the glory of the Lord will protect you
        from behind.
Then when you call, the Lord will answer.
    'Yes, I am here,' he will quickly reply."

I began to think about the growing political divisiveness, social conflicts, the unhealthy power of social media, the growing prevalence of bullying—all the ills and issues that plague our culture, the dynamics in our world that desperately need God's "justice and fairness."

One day, while in this new place of revelation, I sat down in my studio with a renewed sense of intentionality. This time, the result was quite different. Very quickly, God began to speak, melodies began to flow, ideas began to download, and I kept the record button on for hours.

In the time following Dad's passing and prior to this moment of God speaking to me, anything I might have tried to write could have been forced and come from my own ideas. I believe God used the break to get me to a new place. He called me to climb up to a new plateau to see things from a higher point of view. He offered to expand my worldview. He wanted me to be His messenger, not anyone else's, not even my own. He alone is the Creator and the God of the Message. We are simply ambassadors who agree to be vessels, channeling His creativity.

My grief and adjustments to life without Dad, the creative drought, and then my discovery of Amos 5 all culminated in the creation of new music, more new music than I had ever created in such a short time span. From those sessions, I released *A Million Lights*, a pop album where I lyrically addressed cultural issues such as social divisions, suicide, lack of identity, and unforgiveness. The primary message I wanted to communicate through the new songs was that no one, and I mean no one, is here by mistake or random chance. *Every* life has a purpose. There is a plan available from a loving God. But we also have an enemy that wants to steal, kill, and destroy, whose biggest goal is to distort and destroy our view of God as a loving Father.

Once again, I learned that the songwriting process for me is more like *catching* something that falls from Heaven than *calling* on something that comes from me. I just reach out and catch it as it comes down.

Simultaneously with the album *A Million Lights*, I also released *Surrounded*, a worship album. This project was a physical and artistic way to connect my new focus on justice and worship. Two dynamics that must work together in the Kingdom helped me create two projects that work hand in hand to communicate God's truths. I came to the understanding that the style of our expression isn't of much concern to God, but instead that we give Him our hearts, and that we be vulnerable, honest, and humble. As cliché as it might sound, we're to come as we are. Every tribe, every tongue, every social class, every denomination is to come together in community.

To record audio and video of *Surrounded*, rather than the usual setup with me and the band on stage and the people below on the floor, everyone was on the same level. The two-hundred-plus folks we invited stood all around us. They *surrounded* us as we led. God surrounded us all as we worshipped.

In one of the most truly special times I have ever experienced, we captured seventy minutes of worshipping together in authenticity, declaring the promises of God. For me, *Surrounded* was about more than worship, though; it was also about spiritual warfare—the battle being fought in the Heavenly realms every day on our behalf. Like worship and justice, those two concepts also work together.

As God has taught me more and more from His Word, and I have come to understand more of His heart for the world, my goal in being out front in worship is to lead only from my heart, and not from a set list, or people's expectations, or even my own musicality. My desire, even though I am leading, is to disappear. Disappear into the midst of the worshippers. Disappear into the presence and the power of God. As Jesus said in John 3:30, "He must become greater and greater, and I must become less and less."

Most of us who are Christ-followers would likely agree that biblically the Church is actually more responsible for offering solutions for the state of the world than the government. Yet using the term "the Church" makes it sound like a huge organization that can easily be the scapegoat and shoulder our blame. In reality, the Church is *us*, individual believers making up the Body of Christ. Therefore, we can *all* do better. We can *all* take our faith and works, joined together, to another level, toward worship and justice.

Is it too simple to suggest that if we all did *one* random act of kindness every day in Jesus's name, we could make a massive difference in the world?

What if we could all accept our identity in Christ, that we *are* His beloved?

What if we stopped trying to earn grace that we have *already* been given?

He already calls us His own, so the focus is not to be on what we *can* do, but what He *has* done.

Today, my life is not about record sales, video streams, the size of the venues I play, or how many social media followers I acquired this week, but rather about continually maximizing my platform for Christ. Now the reality is that the records, tours, and fans are what built the platform. But now that I have one, I am well aware of the massive responsibility to use it all for . . . *wait for it* . . . worship and justice. Because Jesus taught us in Luke 12:48:

> When someone has been given much, much
> will be required in return; and when someone
> has been entrusted with much, even more will
> be required.

God's revelations, His Word, His blessings, and the realization and responsibility I have been given have driven me to get involved across the globe and right here at home—with Bono in his HIV/AIDS programs in Africa, and then also with Rocketown, our nonprofit youth center in Nashville. The greatest joy of my life is not another music award, but hearing a kid tell me, "I was contemplating suicide, but then I came to Rocketown, heard the truth, and got loved on. They accepted me for who I am and didn't focus on my past. That was a game-changer for me."

The best way we can change the world is one heart, one life at a time. We see in the Gospels that this is exactly what Jesus did. From the guy at the homeless shelter who's felt invisible and unloved for years, to the coworker who's struggling with their marriage, to the neighbor who knows that when you say you'll pray for their family, you actually do. People want to experience authenticity, not celebrity. They desire interaction with integrity, not entertainment. They want to know their lives have a purpose. We have the privilege of sharing the good news that they can know the One who holds their hope and their future.

This is a powerful lesson I learned from my dad's life, from his esteemed reputation back in Kenova to here in Franklin: worship is not about singing a handful of songs once a week, but about our day-in-and-day-out interactions with people, from the living room to the office, from our spouses to the cashier at the convenience store. Worship is not a Sunday morning *event*, but a life *experience*. Worship is our expression of

God's love and life to the world. Justice is joining God in bringing *His* righteousness to the world.

> O people, the LORD has told you what is good,
>    and this is what he requires of you:
> to do what is right, to love mercy,
>    and to walk humbly with your God.
>    (Micah 6:8)

## Chapter Twelve

# Choirs and Crooners

## ❖ The Father's Conversation ❖

One song on my album *A Million Lights* is titled "Conversation." While walking through the very dark and difficult season of 2020, reading the news, watching footage of yet another tragic event, and praying about how to be a part of the solution and not part of the problem, I couldn't stop thinking about this song. Listening to the words on repeat against the backdrop of such a tumultuous year, I decided we needed to create a video to connect powerful visual images to the lyrics of that song, which were now even more timely than the day we released it. The capabilities we have for producing a powerful story through art and media can be such a personal and persuasive way to reach people and touch hearts.

The main line of the chorus is a request we all must make in our circles of influence: "Bring me into the conversation." So much of the communication today is *not* conversation at all, but more confrontation, manipulation, sensation, dictation, litigation, and even damnation. No matter our politics or personal beliefs, we have to listen once again and be open to having some uncomfortable dialogue, even within our own hearts. Throughout the Gospels, we find Jesus reminding us of the state of mind we must have to please Him.

Then Jesus told this story to some who had great confidence in their own righteousness and scorned everyone else: "Two men went to the Temple to pray. One was a Pharisee, and the other was a despised tax collector. The Pharisee stood by himself and prayed this prayer: 'I thank you, God, that I am not like other people—cheaters, sinners, adulterers. I'm certainly not like that tax collector! I fast twice a week, and I give you a tenth of my income.'

"But the tax collector stood at a distance and dared not even lift his eyes to heaven as he prayed. Instead, he beat his chest in sorrow, saying, 'O God, be merciful to me, for I am a sinner.' I tell you, this sinner, not the Pharisee, returned home justified before God. For those who exalt themselves will be humbled, and those who humble themselves will be exalted." (Luke 18:9–14)

In the video for "Conversation," we introduced characters in a montage of difficult moments in life. But then we brought in the reality that when a conversation is actually allowed to take place, a two-way street of respectful and tactful dialogue can happen, resolution can be made possible, and hope has the potential to be established in almost any circumstance.

There seems to be at least a growing understanding through the storms of today that the symptoms of our social ills are many. For example, social media can be fun and informative, but then the dark side of such platforms presents a systemic danger to our culture. Hating what we don't or won't understand has become commonplace and sadly, in many circles, acceptable. One-sided online commentary invites anyone to make judgments about people with little to no knowledge of the actual circumstances. Our culture, especially with social media, would lead us to believe it's acceptable to call anyone who doesn't think like you want them to a bigot. Instead of trying to understand that individual person, we simply apply a label to them and move on.

It's important, though, to look to the other side of our differences. Over the years throughout my career, I have had the privilege of becoming friends with artists from a broad range of musical genres, from the Oak Ridge Boys to the Winans, from Sandi Patty to Jordin Sparks, and from Charlie Daniels to Bono.

I have had the blessing and privilege of

- performing at events and leading worship in Washington, DC, and around the nation, where people from both sides of the aisle were in attendance;
- being invited into rooms in foreign countries with kings, presidents, and dictators who disagreed with the ideals of our country but respected and welcomed my music, even as a man of faith;
- leading worship at conferences where denomi-national leaders who inherently opposed

one another on deep theological issues sang together;

- performing in halls where people of many faiths and beliefs were represented and my songs were received with respect and reverence; and

- presenting livestreaming events where people of varying lifestyles listened intently to my performance.

I have seen over and over again from a front-row seat how people can set aside a Grand Canyon–sized chasm of differences to listen and receive my message as an artist. That is exactly why I know and believe that a *conversation* can take place in even the most unlikely rooms with the most unlikely people. And the goal doesn't have to be winning or changing one another's minds, but rather showing that neither are actually the monsters others once suspected. We might walk in with an attitude and defense and walk away with respect and understanding.

We can love one another in spite of the reasons we can come up with to *not* love one another. First, though, we have to agree to get in the room and have a conversation.

The chaos and division we live in today have brought a new sense of urgency toward action, forcing us to face the world's need for God's hope. As a Christ-follower first, and a musician, singer, songwriter, and actor second, my calling to address the urgent, to stand up and speak up to offer a voice for a Living Hope with real answers only grows stronger as the world spirals downward. For me personally, standing up is sitting down at the piano. My speaking up is through a melody. We each have a responsibility to know how God would have us respond. But we must respond.

I'm going to take a left turn here, but hang with me. I promise I'll come full circle.

Back in my hometown of Kenova, on Sundays at church, my dad always sang in the choir. Standing on the stage with the other singers, he belted out the traditional hymns of the faith and modern Christian songs of the day during our worship services. Dad had a really good voice, sang in key and on pitch, and could navigate any song well.

Then after our family had gotten home and had lunch, Dad would put some "crooner songs" on the record player. He would sing at the top of his voice to Frank Sinatra, Tony Bennett, Bing Crosby, the greats of the day and legends to come. Dad sang all those classic love songs throughout his life. Even when dementia had robbed him of recalling what he just had for lunch, he could sing a classic like "Moon River" or "That's Amore" or "Beyond the Sea," nailing them word for word. My kids all remember hearing Dad sing those classic songs all their lives, right up to his last months.

I believe in a very tangible way Dad showed me throughout his life that there really isn't a line between the sacred and the secular, like we can so easily and often draw. His love of music was a great example. He was the same man of God at home singing Sinatra as he was just hours before singing "Just as I Am." So often the invisible dividing lines laid down that say God is over here in this but He's not over there in that are simply man-made and religion based. Of course, there is a biblical plumb line to be laid down between good and evil, right and wrong. Scripture is clear. But humans have decided on so many of those lines, and too often, *we* are wrong.

*All* of our life is meant to be worship.

All of our life is to be *sacred*.

All of our communication serves us best as a *conversation*.

Everyone who knows anything about me knows I have been a part of the Christian music or gospel music community for thirty-five-plus years, yet in 1991 "Place in This World" "crossed over," and that created some controversy. But I dismissed the comments of "Michael W. Smith is going secular," because to me "Place in This World" is just as biblical and Christ-centered as "Friends." Do they communicate different truths about faith? Well, of course. But every genre of music communicates different aspects of life. Like my dad singing in the choir loft and the living room on Sundays, my heart, goal, and the intent of my music is always the same—to honor God. Sacred.

Have you ever taken a close look at Jesus's conversations in Scripture? From the disciples to the Pharisees, from Nicodemus to the woman at the well, from Satan in the desert to the Father in the Garden, He was sacred in them all. Jesus had a *lot* of conversations, with those who loved Him and those who hated Him. Whether he spoke lovingly or sternly, He spoke from His Father's Spirit.

Have you also ever considered the choices that Jesus had in how to communicate God's truths to us? He was (and is) God, so He could have used *any* method He wanted, from Jedi Mind Control to appearing only at the Temple on the Sabbath and reading from the Torah in a monotone voice. Look at this very interesting passage in the Gospel of Matthew from *The Message* Bible:

> [Jesus asked,] "Are you listening to this? Really listening?"
>
> The disciples came up and asked, "Why do you tell stories?"
>
> He replied, "You've been given insight into God's kingdom. You know how it works. Not everybody has this gift, this insight; it hasn't been given to them. Whenever someone has a ready heart for this, the insights and understandings flow freely. But if there is no readiness, any trace of receptivity soon disappears. That's why I tell stories: to create readiness, to nudge the people toward a welcome awakening. In their present state they can stare till doomsday and not see it, listen till they're blue

in the face and not get it. I don't want Isaiah's forecast repeated all over again:

> Your ears are open but you don't hear a
> thing.
> Your eyes are awake but you don't see
> a thing.
> The people are stupid!
> They stick their fingers in their ears
> so they won't have to listen;
> They screw their eyes shut
> so they won't have to look,
> so they won't have to deal with me
> face-to-face
> and let me heal them.
> (Matthew 13:14–15 MSG)

In short, they *don't* want to have a conversation.

God manifested in human form—Jesus Christ—decided that being a storyteller was the best way to teach and reach people. Did everyone get it? No. In fact, the teachers of the Law hated it. But the common, everyday people? They were drawn in by His simple way of presenting truth.

Today, when someone calls me a pastor, I'll accept that title, when years ago I would have shied away from that description. My calling has always been to follow in His footsteps, provide an atmosphere where God can meet people as I lead worship and be a storyteller. "To create readiness, to nudge the people toward a welcome awakening." To show there really is no dividing line between the sacred and the secular. Because the Father my dad knew, the Father that I know, is there in the midst of it all.

As a storyteller, I want to create a conversation. I want to ask others to bring me into their conversations. I want to invite those who feel like they no longer have a say or have taken themselves out of the conversation to come to the circle, and we will listen.

Those like Ruben in Atlanta.

Like Isaac in South Africa.

And like me at twenty years old when I couldn't see past my guilt and shame.

I want to share what I know would be my Dad's hope for you, and is also my own. The most important conversation you will ever have is with your Abba Father. No matter what kind of earthly dad you had or didn't have. Regardless of that relationship or lack of relationship, God is your Father and wants to know you, love you, and take care of you.

Relevant to this chapter's topic of much-needed conversations is one of the most fascinating verses in all of the Bible is Exodus 33:11.

> The LORD would speak to Moses face to face, as one speaks to a friend. (NIV)

That is exactly what God wants from you. He wants the kind of relationship where He speaks to you face to face, as one speaks to a friend. Not an audible voice, but rather the still, small voice, the gentle whisper, in your heart and spirit. Jesus spoke about the kind of conversation the Father wants to have with you when He said:

> I've told you these things for a purpose: that my joy might be your joy, and your joy wholly mature. This is my command: Love one another the way I loved you. This is the very best way to love. Put your life on the line for your friends. You are my friends when you do the things I command you. I'm no longer

calling you servants because servants don't understand what their master is thinking and planning. No, I've named you friends because I've let you in on everything I've heard from the Father. (John 15:11–15 MSG)

I pray you will join the conversation that your Father wants to have with you as His friend. And then that the connection with Him will drive all your other conversations.

## Chapter Thirteen

# Sugar Cookies and Wiffleball

## ⪻ The Father's Inheritance ⪼

In Deuteronomy 6:5–9, God said the following to His people:

> And you must love the LORD your God with all your heart, all your soul, and all your strength. And you must commit yourselves wholeheartedly to these commands that I am giving you today. Repeat them again and again to your children. Talk about them when you are at home and when you are on the road, when you are going to bed and when you are getting up. Tie them to your hands and wear them on your forehead as reminders. Write them on the doorposts of your house and on your gates.

The act of sharing life and faith from generation to generation is the foundation of biblical tradition, making a relationship with God and His Word a sacred yet normal part of everyday life. Not events, but an experience, a lifestyle. In our family, my mom and dad committed to and accomplished exactly what the verses above said to do. Love God and share Him with your children as you live life. And in their case, also grandchildren and great-grandchildren. For my parents, that life of faith always had a whole lot of love and fun involved, too.

Like so many grandparents, Mom and Dad worked hard to create traditions with all their grandchildren living nearby. One of my kids' favorite memories was making homemade cookies at Mimi and Grandaddy's house for any and every holiday, especially Valentine's Day, Easter, Halloween, and Christmas. All the grandkids looked forward to those days with everyone together in Mimi's kitchen. As more kids were born into the family and her kitchen didn't get any bigger, let's just say, things got a lot messier. *Like, a lot.*

But now that the grandkids are all grown up and started having their own kids, when they reminisce today, they don't necessarily talk about the cookie dough, icing, sprinkles, and the sheer volume of everyone talking at the same time. They all agree on two things: first, the seemingly unending supply of patience Dad had, and second, the certain way he carried himself while not ever saying a word.

During those baking sessions, Dad would stand back, watch everyone, be available to help as needed, and then once the cookies were made and most had been eaten, he would spend the rest of the day cleaning up the kitchen. He wanted Mimi to have the fun of creating with the kids but not have to spend the next few hours cleaning up. And in my dad's usual style, he did it with a smile on his face.

My kids gave my dad a normal, traditional grandfather name—Grandaddy. When my own grandkids came along, I acquired something a bit more, shall we say, nontraditional. They call me G-daddy, an abbreviated and a bit trendier version of my dad's grandparent name. I'm glad I have something more *hip-hop* than *IHOP*.

In talking to my kids about the subject of this book and my relationship with their Grandaddy and our Abba Father, I knew they would all have some things to share. My dad offered his grandchildren and great-grandkids an amazing gift of consistency and presence throughout their raising. Aside from the cookie baking days, here are some of their fondest memories.

## Memory #1—Grandaddy always played with them.

Wiffleball was the sport of choice for many years. They would all go out behind his house and play as long as they could. They never recall my dad ever telling them no when they asked him to play with them. Too busy? No, he always made time. Tired? Back pain? Too hot? Too cold? No, he always said yes, and out they went. Nothing was more important to him than spending time with them. A lot of grandkids out there can recall a time when their grandad came out to play with them, but my kids don't recall *a* time because it was *all* the time. And as they got older, the wiffleball games got more intense.

All those hours of saying yes added up over the years to create a constant example of godly influence. We focus a lot today on quality time in this culture because our quantity is always challenged due to busyness. Dad knew that the best way to influence his grandkids was to offer them both—quantity *and* quality. Mom (Mimi), too.

## Memory #2—Grandaddy gave each of my kids a nickname.

If Dad decided that you were going to be in his inner circle, you were assigned a nickname. So of course, all my kids got nicknames. Terms of endearment. Labels of love. Special, only-for-them-from-him titles. Sometimes they were a derivative of their actual name, and sometimes they had nothing to do with their name at all. He came up with something just for them, and it was one of the many ways he let them know they were unique to him. Even as Dad has gone on to Heaven, I have kept up his practice of calling my kids by those names in private moments.

I sometimes wonder if the practice of giving people nicknames comes from the Bible, where God occasionally changed someone's name. He always had a purpose when He did this, often because of the meaning of the names—old and new. He changed Abram, meaning "exalted father," to Abraham, meaning "father of a multitude or many nations." He changed Jacob to Israel. A really fascinating example was when God changed Sarai, meaning "princess," to Sarah, meaning "*my* princess." Sarah's name change connects to the concept of creating an endearing and personal name for someone you love. Then in the New Testament, Jesus changed Saul to Paul to show his transformation to a new person.

The bottom line of God's new names, or our choosing of personal nicknames, is a sign of a strong relationship and connection. Dad certainly had that with each of my kids, just as I am grateful today as G-daddy to have that with each of my sixteen (and counting) grandkids.

## Memory #3—Grandaddy gave my kids the greatest gift of presence, not presents.

Sure, Grandaddy and Mimi gave gifts, but the best gift was their presence. Ryan, our oldest, can recall going to Kenova when my parents still lived there for Christmas and summer visits. Ryan said,

I can close my eyes and see the layout of their house. I still remember where everything was. Later, as I grew up, I realized Kenova was this very small factory town, but as a kid, I saw it as this beautiful place, this cool little community. I just thought it was awesome. But that was because it was where my grandparents were. We would walk in and see Grandaddy sitting there in his chair. Just his presence was such a constant. You have this idea as a kid that somehow he would just always be in your life. He'll always be there. Because he just always *was*.

My kids also recalled a summer vacation when we all went to the beach in Seaside. One night, they decided to watch the movie *The Truman Show* with Jim Carrey. Grandaddy sat there the entire time with them all, saying nothing. But then when the movie ended, he simply said, "Well, I don't know what that was about." The point to him was not the movie, but being with the kids while they watched a movie.

Dad always loved to sing with the kids, too. He passed on a love of music from generation to generation.

## Memory #4—Grandaddy showed my kids how to love your spouse.

My girls especially recall many moments where they saw true love expressed. They shared,

> A prominent memory is how he treated Mimi. He adored her and showed it consistently. There was one time when we all had lunch together in downtown Franklin. Some of us were going to take Grandaddy home, and some of us were taking Mimi to an appointment. It was just so cute because they had to always kiss goodbye before they left each other, and they would walk and hold hands. We witnessed that all the time, and it reminded us, "You know what? You *can* stay in love with each other." They were obviously each other's best friend.

## Memory #5—Grandaddy and Mimi showed my kids how to love people.

My kids have commented, "I can't imagine anybody coming away and saying they didn't love Mimi and

Grandaddy, because everybody loved them and still continue to love Mimi. A big part of that was their hospitality. They were some of the most welcoming people we've ever known."

"I feel like that was their mission—to make people feel welcome. Mimi even released a cookbook titled *Food That Says Welcome*."

"They were great neighbors. I feel like that's something we aren't very good at anymore in this culture. It's too easy to just do our own thing, but Mimi and Grandaddy knew *everyone* on their street, and everybody loved them. I remember times stopping by their house, and there'd be some random neighbors sitting there having tea with them. There have even been times in years past when they made friends with some of Dad's fans."

"They were just genuinely kind to people. Both Mimi and Grandaddy embodied unconditional love to us. We never heard them judge anybody. Even when there were certain things that we knew they didn't agree with, they would never hold any judgment toward anyone. They were always very, very warm, such servants."

"We always loved going over there, and our kids still love going over there. There's always been something about their home. Something about the atmosphere there that they created together."

"We feel like their number one goal was to just be as 'Jesus' as they could possibly be on this earth. To all of us, they achieved that."

## Memory #6—Grandaddy and Mimi prayed for my kids.

My kids said: "I know Dad attributes his life being saved when he was in his darkest moments to my grandparents' prayers. And I think both he and Mom really adopted that discipline for us, too. What a blessing it is to have godly parents and grandparents praying for us all the time. I know we and our kids have been prayed for since before any of us were born. Because they saw the power of prayer and what it did, they never gave up on praying for us."

We can translate my kids' memories of their Grandaddy into principles for us all to practice in parenting, grandparenting, and all relationships, and especially for me as G-daddy:

1. Balancing quality and quantity time is crucial to grow in love and influence.
2. Creating personalized and unique moments can form a constantly deepening bond.
3. Giving presents is great, but giving presence is the best gift you can ever give.
4. Making your marriage your first priority in love and life is the best example for your kids.
5. Expressing love to others from the heart of Christ is your best witness to the world.
6. Praying is the most proactive expression of love and care you can take for anyone.

The concept of passing down faith on a daily basis to our families was and is evidently very important to God, because just five chapters after that opening quotation from Deuteronomy 6, He offered an almost identical command. I've found over the years that when God repeats Himself in His Word, we should listen closely and obey accordingly, because our faith is the foundation of an inheritance found only in Him.

So commit yourselves wholeheartedly to these words of mine. Tie them to your hands and wear them on your forehead as reminders. Teach them to your children. Talk about them when you are at home and when you are on the road, when you are going to bed and when you are getting up. Write them on the doorposts of your house and on your gates, so that as long as the sky remains above the earth, you and your children may flourish in the land the LORD swore to give your ancestors. (Deuteronomy 11:18–21)

## Chapter Fourteen

# I Release You

### ❮❮ The Father's Home ❯❯

By late 2015 my dad had been in a nearby memory care facility for about a year. He required twenty-four-hour care as the dementia progressed. That November, from the 15th through the 22nd, I was scheduled to play at Jamshil Stadium in Seoul, Smart Araneta Coliseum in the Philippines, MasterCard Grand Theatre in Singapore, and then finish the trip doing a three-day crusade in Tokyo with my close friend and frequent partner in ministry efforts, Franklin Graham. All three nights were at the legendary Budokan with a capacity of 20,000, well known in American music history for being the venue for classic live albums by artists like Bob Dylan and Cheap Trick. Debbie and I would be gone about ten days.

Fortunately, at this point, Dad still recognized me. I could tell he knew who I was. As I always did when I was going on the road, I went to tell him goodbye just before we left. I assured him I would come see him as soon as we got back and tell him all about the trip and what God had done. As always, he was supportive and excited about anything I was going to do.

I had been in Tokyo only six months earlier with Franklin, and while there, I had sensed God was going to do something big in Japan. You could feel the movement of His Spirit in the people. Spiritual momentum. So when these dates were scheduled, I was excited to have the opportunity to go back and be a part of the ongoing work there. I had a strong feeling that this trip would be special in building on what we had experienced before.

Following the other events, right after we had arrived in Tokyo, members of my family began to call to tell us that Dad had developed an infection and taken a turn for the worse, something I always hoped would never happen when I was away, especially when I was on the other side of the world. My manager, Chaz, encouraged me to let him make the arrangements for Debbie and me to fly home right away. The crusade with Franklin was going to begin that night.

I talked to my mom, who to no surprise reassured me, "Michael, you need to do whatever you feel the Lord would have you do. I trust your decision." I knew for a fact that had I been able to speak with my dad, he would have most certainly told me, "Don't you come home, son. You stay and do exactly what God called you there to do."

Needless to say, though, I wrestled with the decision. I remember sitting with Debbie in that hotel room in Tokyo, praying for God to show me what to do. I know in these kinds of circumstances, many people would be quick to advise you to go home and be with your family, while others would say you should put the ministry opportunity first. Until you are actually faced with that situation personally, it is difficult to know what you would do, and I wanted to hear clearly from the Lord and not make a decision based on my own feelings or anyone else's.

After a few hours of praying and listening, I felt a very strong calling and a real peace that I was supposed to stay there for the first night to help set the tone for the three days. Then Debbie and I would leave to go home, and my band, led by Stu G from the legendary group Delirious?, would stay and lead the other two nights. Franklin was gracious and supportive of us leaving the crusade to go home to be with my family.

That first night, the iconic Budokan was packed. Not a seat was left in the house. The expectation and energy of the people were off the charts. When my band and I went out and began to lead worship, immediately the people were engaged. They stood, voices raised, hands in the air, and with each song, the level of intensity grew. I cannot adequately describe what it feels like to be in a room where people are openly loving God, and His love is pouring out in response in a nation that is only 1 percent Christian. Many in that room had brought family, friends, and coworkers for whom they had prayed for years, and now they were about to hear the gospel.

Throughout the songs, I was praying and listening for the Spirit to show me what to do and where to go in the music. In those settings, my job description is clear: set the stage, clear the way, ready the hearts of the people for Franklin Graham to give the gospel. Finally, I decided to close out the time of worship with "Agnus Dei." I thought the Spirit in the room couldn't get any stronger or thicker or closer, but then God turned everything up another notch. When I brought the song to a close and got up from the piano, the massive crowd would not stop singing. They just kept on with the song a cappella.

As I walked off into the side stage and past all of Franklin's support team, all people I know extremely well, they were visibly moved by the response. I walked up the steps to my dressing room, went in, bent over, and put my face in my hands. As the tears began to fall, I could hear the crowd still singing "Agnus Dei," mostly in English, others in their own language.

They sang, "Holy, Holy, are You, Lord God Almighty! . . . Worthy is the Lamb! Worthy is the Lamb!"

It was one of those rare but incredibly special moments when you feel Heaven meets Earth and you get to see a small glimpse of the scene painted for us in Revelation 5 when the Lamb that looked as if it had been slaughtered stood before the throne, took the scroll from the right hand of the One seated on the throne, signifying that the sacrifice for God's people had been made and the work of salvation had been finished for all people for all time.

Alone, listening to the chorus sung again and again, I realized why God had me stay for that first night. In the worship, we could feel something shift. We were fighting a spiritual battle for the city and the nation, with the worshippers out front as warriors. By God's Spirit, not our power or might, we broke through in the Heavenly realms. I believe that movement laid the groundwork for the huge numbers of people who would come to know Christ later that night and the next two as Franklin so simply and profoundly presented the gospel.

Being a part of such a strong movement of God among the people in Tokyo, while at the same time knowing my father was in his final hours back in Tennessee with my family, was a greater emotional battle than I had ever experienced in my life. But that night, Heaven seemed so close I felt like I could touch it, and I finally allowed myself to release all the emotions of the week.

Early the next morning, Debbie and I went to the airport to start the long trip home. As we were waiting for our flight to leave, we found a private spot, and I FaceTimed my dad on my phone. As soon as my family answered, I realized Dad's time was near, and everyone in the family was there except me. They had all gathered around my dad's bed to tell him goodbye.

But in classic Paul Smith fashion, he was still fighting the good fight and hanging on. You know, you often hear about people who somehow wait on the last person in the family to get there before they finally let go. Well, this time, *I* was the last person.

They put the phone up to my dad, and I could see on his face that his time with us was coming to an end. He was at the veil of Heaven, getting ready to cross over, but I knew he could still hear me. I knew what I needed to do. With tears streaming down my face, I said, "Dad, please don't wait on me. You don't need to wait on me. I'll see you on the other side. I release you. I release you. Thanks for being such a great dad. I love you. I love you, Dad." Struggling through my emotions, I must have said, "I release you" at least five times.

Three and a half hours later, while Debbie and I were somewhere over the Pacific Ocean, Dad left this life to be with Jesus. Safe in the arms of Abba, his Father, forever. Fully healed, fully restored, fully present with Christ.

I was able to know beyond any doubt, with absolutely no question, that my dad went to Heaven, in the same way I am confident I will go someday: because of a relationship with God through Jesus Christ. It's the same truth that thousands of people in Tokyo had come to know over those three nights. As John 14:6 states, Jesus "is *the* way, *the* truth, and *the* life" (emphasis added) for all people.

I referenced Revelation 5 earlier and how John saw Jesus in his vision as a slaughtered Lamb. We know that is true because of the brutality of the cross—what was required of Jesus to atone for our sin and redeem our lives. One of the most fascinating accounts in Scripture documenting this moment in history is found in Luke 23.

When Jesus was on the cross hanging between two criminals, we see yet again God's representation and pattern in the power of three, beginning with the Trinity itself. Three men were found guilty and nailed to crosses to pay for their crimes, with one of the most horrific forms of capital punishment ever devised for creating suffering and a slow, agonizing death.

One of the criminals expressed the same hatred for Christ and lack of belief in Him that the religious leaders, the soldiers, and the crowd had shown. The other took a very different stance. Yet these two men, hanging beside the Savior, forever show us the two choices available to everyone throughout history regarding what to do with Jesus Christ.

> One of the criminals hanging beside him scoffed, "So you're the Messiah, are you? Prove it by saving yourself—and us, too, while you're at it!"
>
> But the other criminal protested, "Don't you fear God even when you have been sentenced to die? We deserve to die for our crimes, but this man hasn't done anything wrong." Then he said, "Jesus, remember me when you come into your Kingdom."
>
> And Jesus replied, "I assure you, today you will be with me in paradise." (Luke 23:39–43)

One was full of anger and bitterness, spewing his words of mocking disdain and unbelief. His voice has echoed throughout time to represent those who choose to say no to God's offer of salvation.

The second man was remorseful and repentant. He immediately came to Jesus's defense and declared His innocence. But what he said next got Christ's attention and *also* still rings throughout history as the choice God would have us all make. The man called out to

Jesus by name and expressed great faith by stating he knew Christ had a kingdom and would return there. The amazing thing is he didn't actually ask for salvation. In fact, his words sounded more like, "Please, don't forget about me."

Imagine being that thief, believing you are beyond being saved by anyone, and hearing Jesus promise, "I assure you, today you will be with me in paradise." Today! Paradise! What an amazing exchange of such eternal significance in so few words.

The beauty and power of the gospel lies in the fact that Jesus died for the guilty on *both* sides of Him. Both had a choice in how to respond. Like all people in every generation, there is the opportunity to accept or reject.

Jesus never responded to the first criminal's hate-filled insults. He also didn't curse him or hurt him. He only responded to the one who expressed faith. The bottom line is that salvation can only come through surrender. The intent of the heart is far more crucial than the choice of words. The right phrase does not save; Jesus does.

There is no magic formula, only a merciful Father.

And at eighty-two years old on November 20, 2015, my dad met Him, face to face.

But let me reveal to you a wonderful secret. We will not all die, but we will all be transformed! It will happen in a moment, in the blink of an eye, when the last trumpet is blown. For when the trumpet sounds, those who have died will be raised to live forever. And we who are living will also be transformed. For our dying bodies must be transformed into bodies that will never die; our mortal bodies must be transformed into immortal bodies.

Then, when our dying bodies have been transformed into bodies that will never die, this Scripture will be fulfilled:

"Death is swallowed up in victory.
O death, where is your victory?
   O death, where is your sting?"

For sin is the sting that results in death, and the law gives sin its power. But thank God! He gives us victory over sin and death through our Lord Jesus Christ. (1 Corinthians 15:51–57)

*Chapter Fifteen*

# You Are a Masterpiece

✦ The Father's Offer ✦

So many today, desperate to find answers, are asking the tough questions about life, like:

- Is this really all there is?
- Does my life matter?
- What am I doing here?
- How can I find purpose in my life?

Well, here's a very different question for you: Have you ever wondered why you have fingerprints? Over the years, scientists have released numerous research reports and studies on this mystery of our anatomy, yet they all conflict with or even refute one another. The one truth that science *does* agree on is that no two people on the earth have ever had the same fingerprints.

There has never been a duplicate set found among the millions upon millions of people who have lived on this planet. How could science ever explain that fact, especially if one's origin belief is evolution or random chance?

The only explanation that solves the enigma of fingerprints is the intentional creation of life from a loving Father. The belief that He uniquely made only *one* of you. The old saying, "When God made you, He broke the mold," is partially true. He did make you, but there is no mold, because you are an original! No one has ever existed, or will ever exist, with your looks, personality, gifts, skills, and spirit. That means no one else can fill your place! No one can ever fulfill your life's mission but you!

What if, like the painter's final brush strokes on the canvas, your Father completed you with His customized signature? What if your Abba Father gave you your fingerprints simply to provide clear evidence of the great detail and care He took in your creation?

Some of our biggest struggles throughout life center around two factors: identity and approval. The concept of random chance offers no unique identity. An unknown origin leaves no answers, only questions.

Such a belief leaves approval up to everyone and no one at the same time, which is our current state, wherein the masses seek approval from total strangers online.

But believing in creation by a loving and intentional Father means He gave you your identity so who you are can be found in a relationship with Him through Christ. And with His identity confirmed in you, the only approval needed is to be who you were made to be by the One who made you!

I shared earlier how many years ago as a young man I felt lost and confused in my identity, and was looking for approval in all the wrong places. When I finally realized that Jesus was who He said He was, I received the truth that the God of the universe created me, chose me, saved me, and accepted me. He was all I needed to discover my path and purpose in life. The stories I have told throughout this book provide plenty of evidence of that truth.

Years ago, I received a deep conviction that part of my life's message was to convey in every way possible, through songs, teaching, and acting, that the Father chose you. He wants to save you. He wants you to know you are accepted by Him, and yes, that *He* gave you your fingerprints. The Father alone knows your purpose and the plan for your life. Jeremiah 29:11 is true for *you*:

> "For I know the plans I have for you," declares the LORD, "plans to prosper you and not to harm you, plans to give you hope and a future." (NIV)

In my concerts, I have often recited passages from Psalm 139 from memory, a chapter written so powerfully and poetically by the greatest songwriter in history, David. Right now, whether you think you know this chapter well or you have never heard it before, I invite you to personalize the words to be about *you*. Just as I did, I want you to receive the truth that this was written about you and for you. I want these words to go down deep into your spirit for you to experience the identity and approval that God the Father and Creator offers. If at all possible, read these verses aloud so you can both speak and hear the truth about you.

> O Lord, you have searched me
> and you know me.
> You know when I sit and when I rise.
> You perceive my thoughts from afar.

You discern my going out and my lying down,
  and you are familiar with all of my ways.
And before a word is on my tongue,
  you know it completely.
You hem me in behind and before,
  and you have laid your hand upon me.
Such knowledge is too wonderful for me,
  too lofty for me to attain.

So where can I go from your Spirit?
    Where can I flee from your presence?
If I go up to the heavens, you are there;
    if I make my bed in the depths, you are
      there too.
Or if I rise on the wings of the dawn,
    or settle way on the far side of the sea,
even there your hand will guide me,
    your right hand will hold me fast.
But if I say, "Surely the darkness will hide me
    and the light become night around me,"
even the darkness will not be dark to you;
    the night will shine like the day,
    for darkness is as light to you.

For you created my inmost being;
    and you knit me together in my mother's
        womb.
I praise you, oh God, for I am fearfully and
        wonderfully made;
    your works are wonderful,
    and I know that full well.
My frame was not hidden from you
    when I was made in the secret place,
    when I was woven together in the depths
        of the earth.
Your eyes saw my unformed body;
    all the days ordained for me were written
        in your book
    before one of them came to be.
How precious are your thoughts about me, O
    God!
    How vast is the sum of them!
And if I were to count them,
    they would outnumber the grains of the
        sand. . . .
Search me, God, and know my heart;
    test me and know my anxious thoughts.
And see if there is any offensive way in me,

and lead me in the way everlasting.
(vv. 1–18, 23–24, personally adapted
from NIV)

I want you to turn both your hands palms up and take a close look at your fingerprints, personal evidence that your Father made you. Like my dad said about me from the back of that ambulance to the first responders and all his neighbors, God looks at you and declares, "You know who that is right there? That's my son! That's my daughter! Look how wonderfully complex! My workmanship is marvelous! My thoughts of him or her are precious and outnumber the grains of sand on the shore! I even signed him or her with my own hand with a unique, one-of-a-kind identity. I approve of him or her. My masterpiece!"

Following my dad's departure from this earth to cross over to the other side, I knew one day I would tell this story and offer some of what I've learned from him throughout my life. To express how I got to see some of what Abba Father looks like and speaks like and acts like from watching my dad. To share some of the biblical principles and virtues of my dad that have inspired, encouraged, and challenged me all my life and still do every single day.

And I know that Dad would speak these words with me over you as we end our time together:

> We hope that you will let Him love you.
> We pray that you will let Him father you.
> To receive Psalm 139 as a personal love letter
>     to you.
> To accept His offer of identity and approval
>     that He created you to experience.
> To come to know the truth Paul shared in
>     Romans 8:10–11:

> It stands to reason, doesn't it, that if the alive-and-present God who raised Jesus from the dead moves into your life, he'll do the same thing in you that he did in Jesus, bringing you alive to himself? When God lives and breathes in you (and he does, as surely as he did in Jesus), you are delivered from that dead life. With his Spirit living in you, your body will be as alive as Christ's! (MSG)

If you've never had an encounter with the Living Hope, the alive-and-present God, Abba Father, my prayer is that He will meet you right where you are, right now. That you have that same wake-up call, the same personal revelation that I had many years ago. To come and see He really is the Messiah.

And with that truth alive in your life, you and your Father together can change the world!

# ACKNOWLEDGMENTS

I want to express my love, deep gratitude,
and honor to my family:
My mom, Barbara
My wife, Debbie
My kids: Ryan, Whitney, Tyler, Anna, and Emily
My sister, Kim, and her family: David, Mary Claire,
Caroline, and Sarah Kate
All our grandkids!

# ABOUT THE AUTHORS

**Michael W. Smith,** a multi-platinum recording artist, has won three GRAMMY Awards, forty-five Dove Awards, and an American Music Award, and has sold more than fifteen million albums. He has also given back to the global community, having raised funds to battle AIDS in Africa alongside U2's Bono; started Rocketown, a safe haven for young people in Tennessee to meet and find hope; and helped to improve more than 83,000 children's lives through Compassion International. With a career spanning more than four decades, Smith has acted in and scored multiple films and written fourteen books, including a children's book series. He lives with his wife, Debbie, in Franklin, Tennessee. They have five adult children and sixteen grandchildren.

Find out more about Michael at MichaelWSmith.com.

❀❀    ❀❀

**Robert Noland** spent ten years as a touring musician, songwriter, and producer in Christian music and then twenty years running a para-church ministry where he first began writing Christian resources. Since 2014, he has become a best-selling author, writer, and creative consultant based outside of Franklin, Tennessee.

Find out more about Robert at RobertNoland.com.

MICHAEL W SMITH

# "IN HIS OWN WORDS"

## A TALK THAT INSPIRED THE BOOK

LISTEN NOW
SCAN HERE WITH YOUR SMARTPHONE CAMERA AND FOLLOW THE LINK.

# HERE ARE MORE GREAT WAYS TO BE ENCOURAGED EVERYWHERE YOU GO!